PENNSYLVANIA DUTCH
AMERICAN FOLK ART

PENNSYLVANIA
DUTCH
AMERICAN
FOLK ART

Henry Kauffman

DOVER PUBLICATIONS, INC.
New York

Copyright © 1946 by Henry J. Kauffman
Copyright © 1964 by Dover Publications, Inc.
All rights reserved under Pan American and International Copyright Conventions.

Published in the United Kingdom by Constable and Company, Limited, 10 Orange Street, London W.C.2.

This Dover edition, first published in 1964, is a revised and enlarged version of the work first published by American Studio Books in 1946.

Library of Congress Catalog Card Number: 64-13462

Manufactured in the United States of America

Dover Publications, Inc.
180 Varick Street
New York 14, N.Y.

To B. N. O.

who came to Pennsylvania from the Midwest to teach Pennsylvanians of their heritage

ACKNOWLEDGMENTS

The author and publishers wish to express their sincere thanks to the Museums and private collectors who have so generously loaned material from their collections for illustration in this book. Thanks are also due to Mrs. Naaman Keyser for her help in preparing the text, and to Zoe Elizabeth Kauffman for the line drawings on the text pages.

CONTENTS

INTRODUCTION

The purpose of this introduction is to re-introduce the folk art of a group of European people who started their immigration into America at the end of the 17th Century.

All along the Eastern seaboard of the North American continent are evidences of similar immigrations, many of which contributed richly to the early history of this country. But the purpose of this introduction and in fact, the whole book, is to focus attention upon a small district in this vast continent which contributed more than any other community to the folk art of early America—the German counties of Pennsylvania—better known as the "Land of the Pennsylvania Dutch."

The wave of immigration from the countries of North Europe brought with it an interesting pattern in the various forms of items of household equipment. These objects, for the most part, still answer the purpose for which they were made as well as, and often better than, the utensils we now create with the aid of better tools and machinery. Furthermore, they possess individuality and a charm which comes from the manner in which they are decorated.

Such impressions meet the eye at first glance. As we look at them again, we find that they hold for us still another story, for they speak eloquently of those far-off days near the beginning of the world's greatest human experiment. In order to survive in those days, one had to possess a special kind of toughness born of resistance to the elements and a determination to adapt oneself to the different conditions of life peculiar to a new country. In the early rough and ready wooden houses, one sees attention directed to the necessities of life and then, only when time permitted, a little decoration is allowed to relieve the tired aesthetic sense. Whether they be dwellings, furniture or utensils, we may fancy we can see in them something of the character of their creators, for in spite of their various graces, there always appears that essential toughness which was so much a part of the life to which they contributed.

Their creators were, for the most part, what we should call "amateurs," handy with saw, axe and chisel, and able to control a paint brush. They were also possessed of a lot of hope. So it was that with the beginning of a new life in a new country came the expression of a new art based on the traditions and experiences of the Old World but toughened by the conditions of the New.

A considerable number of Americans today have an appreciation of this early form of folk art, not merely from the point of view of a collector of rare items, but for the idea behind it all. The result is that many items of Pennsylvania Dutch Folk Art— the subject with which we specifically deal—have been rescued from oblivion and destruction and valuable private and public collections of them have been made. Unfortunately, in a single volume, space only allows the mention (in appropriate places throughout this book) of but comparatively few of the names of private individuals and public institutions who have done such splendid work in the interest of instruction, entertainment and inspiration of posterity.

We may wonder why it has taken so long to appreciate a folk art so closely bound up with the early life of America. To some extent, the answer may be contained in the remark which was made only recently by an elderly descendent of a Pennsylvania Dutch family, "What they find in those things, I don't know. I've been throwing them away all my life and now it seems folks will pay almost anything for some bit of a painted tin or a cracked pie dish."

During the successive stages necessary to the evolution from one state to another, considerations of one generation might seem important to the special circumstances of its time, but, by the next generation, they may be thought quite unimportant because a new set of circumstances has in the meantime arisen. While there are forests to be cleared before the plough can be used, the work of felling trees is all important. When the forests are cleared, tree felling is of little importance to the ploughman.

So it was with Pennsylvania Dutch Folk Art. The coming of power machinery encouraged people to buy the cheaper, though flimsier, household goods and to discard, as being too homely, the old equipment which had done such good work in the past. It is only now, after a period of latent interest, that we seek again those things which possess such striking individuality. The craftsmanship of the past is still on view for everyone to see in its primitive beauty and tough virtuosity—an unfinished art waiting to play its part again in the days to come. Some day, after more trials and setbacks, we shall again start to "make the most splendid race the sun ever shone upon." The flowers that will be needed in the great period of art attendant on this race grow upon such ground as was prepared by these early Pennsylvania Dutch.

C. G. H.

THE HISTORICAL BACKGROUND OF THE PENNSYLVANIA DUTCH

Unfortunately, there is much controversy among informed people about Pennsylvania Dutch Art, its European origin, terminology and sources of inspiration, for the simple reason that comparatively little documentary evidence exists. The issue is further confused by the fact that many pieces credited to American craftsmanship were in actual fact brought from Europe by the early settlers. For a long time, little attention was given either to the history or craftsmanship of the Pennsylvania Dutch, and many who did have accurate information failed to record it. However, fragmentary documentation is to be found which, when joined with the authentic examples of craftsmanship that we still have today, forms a general pattern like separate squares of a patchwork quilt.

In any appreciation of the art of the Pennsylvania Dutch, a brief outline of the background of the early immigrants, so far as it is known, and the conditions under which they started a new life in America, seems necessary to record before dealing more specifically with a native craftsmanship so obviously conditioned by these factors.

It appears fairly certain that the first Germanic immigrants to come to America and settle in what is now known as Germantown, were a comparatively wealthy class of craftsmen from the area of Crefeld. The natural prosperity they achieved in a new and fertile territory resulted in glowing letters sent back to Europe telling relatives and friends of the political and religious freedom, as well as the great opportunities of financial independence that were to be had in the New World. Evidently they made little mention of the extreme ordeals of travel and ignored the hard struggle, if not servitude, that the less fortunate who were unable to pay their transportation in advance would probably have to face for many years to come. There were undoubtedly, however, many thousands of poorer peasants prepared to risk hardships in the belief that conditions would prove no worse than those at home, and with the newly fostered belief that eventually freedom would be theirs. The English shipping agents, who went down the Rhine encouraging the peasants to emigrate to America, undoubtedly had nothing more in mind than the collection of substantial sums for their transport. The crowded and unsanitary conditions of the ships were unspeakable, but these conditions, at least comparatively short-lived, must have been preferable to the prolonged ordeals of war, religious persecution, and abuse at the hands of civil authorities, which were prevalent in Europe at the time. Most of the early settlers of the Pennsylvania Dutch region are believed to have come from the Palatinate region of Germany and its vicinity, though other territory officially listed includes the Lower Rhine, Alsace-Lorraine, Switzerland, Silesia, Saxony and Moravia. Upon arrival in this country, many were diverted by the British to a section of New York called Schoharie Valley. Others landing in South Carolina, New Jersey and Maryland, are believed to have gravitated toward Pennsylvania, where the influx of Palatinates eventually became so great, that after the year 1727, all in Philadelphia were required to sign the ships' register as well as to swear allegiance to the British Crown. As the boats brought in

9

more and more cargoes of these ill-looking and ragged peasants, the Quakers began to fear that if some measure of control was not exercised they would themselves be outnumbered and thereby lose control of the affairs of the province, specifically planned by William Penn as a refuge for those of Quaker faith. Therefore, probably only the indentured were permitted to stay in the Philadelphia area, while the majority of the others fanned out into land now forming the counties of Berks, Lehigh, Lebanon, Dauphin, Lancaster and York. Between 40,000 and 65,000 immigrants from Germany arrived in Philadelphia between the years 1727 and 1775. This mass migration must have brought a wide cross-section of people. Some say that the jails were cleared in Germany, others stress the poverty of the peasants, while still others concede that many were holders of college degrees or were skilled craftsmen. Probably, all this is partly true, but the interesting fact remains that out of the mixed group emerged a surprisingly simple and pious people with a desire to live according to their particular interpretations of the Bible. On the whole, too, they possessed an obstinate determination to win against what must have appeared to many as unconquerable odds, despite the glowing prospects that had been presented to them in Europe by those who had migrated. It is also extraordinary that against such a background as theirs there should have emerged so decisive a faculty for craftsmanship—more prolific and reaching greater heights than that of any other early American community.

Among the religious groups first represented in the province, besides the Quakers, were the Mennonites, the Moravians, the Dunkers, the Ephrata Pietists, also members of the Church of England and of the Lutheran, Presbyterian, and Reformed congregations. Much publicity has been given to the groups who seemed to deviate from the American norm, but it should also be pointed out that a large percentage of the early immigrants were, as many of the present inhabitants still are, members of Lutheran and Reformed churches. Actually, people of the Reformed and Lutheran faiths came chiefly to participate in the economic freedom that had been denied them in Europe, rather than for reasons of religious freedom, for along with the Roman Catholics, their faiths had been recognized by the Treaty of Westphalia.

As already suggested, all the groups who came to live in what was called "Penn's Holy Experiment" held strong religious convictions. In the earliest days, services were held in the houses and barns of the congregation, and this practice is still sometimes adhered to today. After the first necessity of building log houses had been attended to, the community usually pooled its resources for the building of a place of worship. The early churches had no floors and the benches for the congregation were made of roughly hewn wood. It appears that probably a raised platform was erected at the front of the building, on which stood a table to serve as a pulpit. As there were no heating devices, it was customary to build a fire outside the church, where the congregation gathered to warm themselves before entering. Because of the lack of ordained ministers, the leadership of the church was provided for by drafting lay members or employing the local schoolteacher. Sermons were measured by hour glasses, the usual length being from one to two hours, undoubtedly with a proportionately long time for prayer. It was customary also for families to give part of their day to worshiping at home. Sunday, of course, was the most important day of the week. Only necessary work was done in the house, the remainder of the day being devoted to meditating or attending church. No member of the family was permitted to work except the mother, who on the other hand, assisted by a grown daughter, was expected to cook the most elaborate meal of the week.

The German language was most common among these immigrants and, therefore, it was principally used in church. Many congregations, especially the Reformed and Lutheran, cooperated with the Church of England. Gradually, as the children began to learn English, demands were made that English be used in German churches. This condition, at first, was difficult to meet, for the older and more conservative elements wished to retain their native language. A compromise was eventually reached by holding one service in German and one in English. Only a short step then remained to an all-English service.

Like the present-day Amish, the early settlers of the region were mostly farmers. To some extent, this meant that they were also craftsmen, for there were such things on the farm as wheelbands to be welded, carpentry of a crude sort to be done, harnesses to be repaired and so on. Besides farming and carpentry, forestry was one of the important skills that was necessary in the New World and was, in fact, an obvious preliminary to the building of houses and the cultivating of farmland.

At the beginning, farm crops were not rotated and the land was soon drained of its fertility. The land then had to lie fallow for as many years as were required to restore its fertility. While uncleared land was plentiful, new fields were always cleared, but when the farmer was limited in land, he then resorted to the scientific rotation of crops. Attempts of vintners, who were among the groups that came to the region, were not successful due to the unsuitability of the land to viticulture, and they resorted instead to the raising of wheat. Fruit was also grown and the well regulated farm always had an apple orchard.

The families of the early Pennsylvania Dutch were usually large, often consisting of ten children. Parents and grandparents frequently lived with the younger members of the family and sometimes a small addition was built onto the house for them.

The father was the unquestioned head of the family and conducted all matters of business. The education of the children was also his responsibility, particularly the boys. In business or on the farm, the boys were usually apprenticed to their father or to an intimate friend. On the farm they made themselves useful in such ways as carrying food and water to the workers in the field, washing cattle in unfenced areas and caring for the chickens and other fowl. The girls' job was to assist their mother with milking, making butter, sewing, caring for the flowers, baking and keeping the house clean. An older girl's achievement in these matters was of proverbial importance to her suitor when he considered her as a prospective bride. The Pennsylvania Dutch have always been famous for their well kept houses and barns. It was just as important that the feeding entries in the barn were well swept, the horses curried, the stables kept clean as it was for the cellars in the house to be whitewashed, the steps and floors scrubbed, the cutlery polished and the furniture kept spotlessly clean.

In the life of the Pennsylvania Dutch, births were quite unimportant affairs. Weddings, on the contrary, were worthy of great celebrations and death brought the usual share of mourning and gossip. After a burial, the mourners returned either to the church or to the home of the deceased where neighboring women provided an immense spreading of food. Then groups would eat in relays, for there was never room for all to be seated at one time. This arrangement was popular, as those who were not eating had plenty of time to discuss politics, the weather, crops, not to mention the financial resources of the deceased. Undoubtedly, however, there were some among them who took the occasion less lightly. Great distances, at times extending over an entire county, were travelled by horse and carriage on such occasions.

Of course, the colonial life of these people was, like the lives of settlers in other parts of the country, harried by the Indians against whom they had to be constantly on guard. To begin with, also, they had the discomfort of being misunderstood by other groups who interpreted their love of their native language and their European customs as marks of disloyalty. However, time gradually healed these differences and the English, Irish, Scotch, French, Dutch, Germans and Swiss learned the necessity of living together as friendly and useful neighbors. The intermarriage of nationalities made the fusion more complete and permanent, resulting in an American people still known as the Pennsylvania Dutch.

THE ART OF THE PENNSYLVANIA DUTCH

The building of the sturdy and attractive houses of the Pennsylvania Dutch settlers in the limestone valleys between the Schuykill and the Susquehanna resulted from their newly won feeling of freedom and the knowledge that their descendents would prosper in the New World.

Most of the early objects of the Pennsylvania Dutch were purely utilitarian in purpose and appearance, but as living conditions gradually became easier for these people, they began to recreate the decorative furniture and patterns that were characteristic of their early homeland. Their art was to some extent a fusion of many designs and motifs which originated in scattered parts of Germany and Central Europe and which were continually renewed by craftsmen arriving from the Old World. The tendency, through necessary economy of both time and money, was to simplify these designs and, of course, to adapt them to the native materials of Pennsylvania, with the result that they have character of their own, however closely associated they may be with European design.

At the peak of their creative period, which was the first half of the 19th Century, the Pennsylvania Dutch decorated their houses with colorful furnishings which became an integral part of their daily lives and surroundings. The decorations in each house were a personal reflection of the family. Furniture always had an individual touch. The dower chests, spoon racks, children's toys, cradles and small chairs contributed to the picture they have left us of a happy, industrious and religious people who loved their homes and lived in an atmosphere of mutual affection.

The decorative patterns and unsophisticated designs, so distinctive of Pennsylvania Dutch folk art, have greatly endeared them to the contemporary American taste. Although domestic craftsmanship abounded in the vicinity, it must be remembered that the district itself was comparatively small, so that the quantity of painted chests and furniture of all kinds, also of pottery, glass, woven coverlets, cross-stitched samplers and fractur was definitely limited, making original pieces quite rare today.

Few of the Pennsylvania Dutch motifs can be said to have been of strictly American origin. In most instances, the source was in nature, history or religion and, by and large, the immigrant copied in America what had already been done in his European homeland, adding here and there personal touches of his own. Sometimes, however, designs were influenced by the new surroundings and the culture and history of the New World.

The tulip was one of the most frequently used motifs. This flower had been brought to Europe from Asia Minor about the middle of the 16th Century. Immediately, it gained much popularity, spreading further north to the gardens of England as well as Germany and the Low Countries. The bulbs became an item of commerce and the fortunes of merchants rose and diminished as the fashion fluctuated. In his book, "The Tulip Ware of the Pennsylvania German Potters," Barber states that, "The Tulipenwuth, or tulip-madness, extended into Germany and continued to rage for many years. The German potters of the 18th Century, particularly throughout the Rhenish Palatinate, used the tulip extensively as a decorative subject on their slip-decorated earthenware." The tulip, also widely grown in Pennsylvania, must have been a constant reminder of its European use in peasant design and the simple outline of the flower made it suitable for untrained as well as trained hands to execute. Most authorities believe that the tulip had a religious meaning, the presence of three flowers symbolizing the Trinity. Wertenbaker, in his book, "The Founding of American Civilization, The Middle Colonies," states that the tulip was "accepted in Germany as a variation of the Holy Lily." This being the case, it is easy to understand its prominence in the art of so strongly religious a people as the Pennsylvania Dutch.

Other flowers such as the rose, fuchsia, forget-me-not, violet and the lily, and fruits such as the pomegranate and grape, both in natural and conventionalized forms, were also used as motifs for all forms of decoration. Almost as popular as the flower was the bird motif. In later examples, the eagle was frequently chosen, not only because it was a native bird, but also because of its special association with the country's newly won independence. The eagle often formed the major part of trade marks used by the pewter craftsmen. William Will, a pewterer of German birth, was one of the first to use the eagle touch. After the American Revolution, eagle touches were extremely common and, in the first decades of the 19th Century, they were used in Philadelphia by Plumly and Bidgood, Parks Boyd, Barnes and the Palethorpes. The different birds found in the neighborhood were a constant source of inspiration. The pelican appeared on pottery pie plates, the dove on manuscripts, the swan on butter molds, the rooster on glassware and the peacock on textiles and needlework. The peacock is also the central theme of sgraffito plates and jars made by George Hubener. Other bird motifs were the parrot, chanticleer, scarlet tanager, yellow warbler, and the "distelfink."

Human figures and animals also abound in all media of the Pennsylvania Dutch. Mounted horsemen are found on sgraffito ware; children, unicorns and lions on birth certificates or chests; deer on pottery, and rabbits, hares and hounds on enameled pieces of Stiegel type glassware. It is in the motifs of historical derivation that human figures were mostly used. David Spinner made a sgraffito pie plate showing a

13

man and a woman in typical colonial costumes. Another sgraffito plate shows British officers dancing with colonial dames to the tune of a fiddle. Johannes Neesz expressed his patriotism by using General Washington on horseback for one of his sgraffito plates. General Washington was also known to have been used on the lids of brides' boxes. Some of these boxes, not influenced by early American history, or at any rate not obviously so, have only brides as their motif while others have a bride and groom fully dressed for the marriage ceremony. In the case of the latter, the inscription around the edge carries the simple sentiment, "Your heart and my heart are as one." Other examples of historical subjects are the flag of the United States and the capitol building at Washington which exist on later pieces.

It was on the cast iron stove plates that religion was most intimately intermingled with art in Pennsylvania. It is difficult to ascertain definitely whether the early stove plates were imported or cast from imported patterns, but in any event they were widely used in the homes of the Pennsylvania Dutch. So frequently do biblical scenes and characters appear on the plates that a publication of the Bucks County Historical Society is called "The Bible in Iron." Until the year 1750, most of the decorative patterns bore such inscriptions as Mary and Martha, Cain and Abel, The Flight into Egypt, The Miracle of Cana, David and Goliath, and The Pharisee and The Publican. After 1750, the religious motto or quotation was retained but a conventionalized floral pattern was substituted for the previously used biblical scene. The "Bible in Iron" explains that "this sudden innovation in design, which can be described as a theme of decoration endlessly repeated with slight variations, but never duplicated, consists of an upper panel showing the chief floral design, a central panel or cartouche with the inscription, and a lower panel with a medallion generally containing the date. An upper panel, still framed with the familiar vaulted canopies of the pictorial plate no longer encloses a pictorial subject, but a set pattern, either half of which serves for the front plate, the pattern appearing in full on the side. This consists of a flowerpot growing a tulip plant, generally balanced with lozenges, six point stars and frequently what appear to be sheaves of wheat in the right canopy. Almost invariably after 1755, in the left canopy, a fluted circlet appears which may represent an aureole with divergent rays enclosing a heart from which spring several tulips. This rests upon what seems to be a stand formed of the heads and forelegs of sheep." In this manner, religion and art were closely interwoven into their daily lives like weft threads on the warp. The angels that appeared on the brides' boxes and manuscripts and the other motifs with religious connotations such as the lamb, the dove, the pelican, the heart, the cross, the crown and the sun, moon and stars were yet other manifestations of the same idea.

When speaking of Pennsylvania Dutch Art, we think of the years between 1750 and 1850, for it was especially then that the spirit of craftsmanship, now almost vanished, flowered in the counties from Bucks to York. These craftsmen were not the outgrowth of a school or an academy, nor did they for the most part spend years in formal apprenticeship. The inspiration came from the home itself and from the work of their parents and grandparents. Although the products were for home use, and in many cases were actually made there, it may be supposed that the better craftsmen made more than their immediate families needed and therefore many such articles must have been sold or bartered.

Besides the family craftsman, many of the most skilled workers became professionals and worked in such popular local industries as pottery, weaving, carpentry, masonry, building and glassmaking. There were also blacksmiths (who did all manner of wrought iron work), saddlers and wheelwrights. Eventually too, the printing trade needed skilled labor of a different sort. Many of these separate crafts are dealt with individually on the succeeding pages, but a few miscellaneous examples of early professional workmanship, which contributed so greatly to the local color of early times, should be mentioned if only briefly. For instance, there were the wheelwrights and blacksmiths who combined their skills to produce the famous Conestoga wagons, which were the means of commercial transportation in the colonial days. They were beautifully made of hickory, oak and poplar wood, and skillfully reinforced with bands and corner braces of forged iron. The red and blue wagons must have been a picturesque sight as they travelled the great Lancaster turnpike, their white tops flapping in the wind.

In Lancaster, the Kentucky rifle reached its highest stage of development. This masterpiece was the product of the gunsmith and the woodworker. It had a long rifled, octagonal barrel, and its maple stocks were often made of curly maple and decorated with silver and brass. The patch boxes were beautifully engraved, the hinges cleverly fitted, and sometimes squirrels were perched on the end as finials.

Although the famous Sauer press was owned by one man, its products resulted from the efforts of many. This press was the first to print the German language in the New World. It is particularly well-known for its almanac, for its newspaper which was circulated throughout the colonies, and also, of course, for the Sauer Bible. Contemporary with the Sauer Press was the one operated by the Ephrata Pietists who aided Sauer in the printing and binding of his Bible. Besides being the first group to print in both the German and English languages in America, the monastic colony at Ephrata is famous for its publication of the "Martyr's Mirror" (1748), for which they employed their own craftsmen for setting type and printing, their own leather tanners for the bindings, and special metal workers for making the clasps. The female members of this religious community were well-known for their lettering and illumination, which can be seen at the relics of their dwelling on the banks of the Cocalico.

In conclusion, it is perhaps interesting to observe that in the Pennsylvania Dutch country today one can still find native craftsmen. There are farmers who make combs of cattle horns in their spare time, others who carve wood and who make baskets, women who hook and braid rugs, make quilts and embroider. There is also an undertaker who paints furniture in his spare time. Several are known to me personally, and there must be dozens more, to encourage us in the belief that the craftsmanship of the Pennsylvania Dutch yet lives, while the art of their past assumes ever greater importance in the contemporary study of early American folk art.

ARCHITECTURE

Travelling in the land of the Pennsylvania Dutch today, the first thing we see is their architecture. The houses and large farm buildings are usually situated a short distance from the highway, surrounded by many acres of limestone land. The house is characteristic of the region, but is not as easily identified as the huge Swiss barns that are so famous. The city of Lancaster is particularly noted for its red brick houses while the beautifully styled and solidly constructed stone houses are typical of the Oley Valley.

Little evidence is found today of the log houses that were built by the early settlers. These were extremely interesting from the point of view of construction. Dr. Henry C. Mercer, in his monograph "The Origin of Log Houses in the United States," points out that the Swedish people had built log houses in the Delaware Valley before the English arrived there. These buildings were rectangular in shape, either with or without cellars. They contained a stone fireplace at the end of the two-room house, or in the center of the four-room house. The second floor, or loft, was supported by timbers roughly hewn on two sides and inserted in notches cut into the logs of the side wall. Although many cabins were hurriedly and crudely built, none of the logs used were notched at the top, as this would have formed a water pocket and would have resulted in subsequent disintegration of the corner. Very often the logs were left round and were roughly notched near the end for overlapping. This method required much chinking and was only used when the building was built as a temporary dwelling place. Other examples have been found where the logs were carefully squared, notched and chamfered, thus making a more satisfactory corner and, at the same time, throwing the water away from the house.

The log cabin was extremely rare in England and the English, therefore, followed the practice of the Swedish or else built houses of clapboard. For this type of house, the boards were split into five or six foot lengths and shaved thin with a large knife. They were then fastened to a previously built framework of rough timber with some overlapping of the boards to give better protection from the weather. Because of the rough fitting of the boards, it was sometimes necessary to plaster the houses on the inside. In contrast to the English, many of the German immigrants, who were familiar with the log houses of the Black Forest or of Switzerland, were able to build very good examples in Pennsylvania. In the cabins they erected, the logs were carefully squared and the corner notches were made to resemble a dovetail joint. This added strength to the construction and reduced the amount of chinking required for weatherproofing. The chimney was usually in the center and the gable end above the first floor was covered with vertical boarding. There was, of course, a considerable overlapping of architectural styles in this region, as was true in other parts of the country, due to the different influences that came with the mixed nationalities of the early immigrants and the English colonists.

Perhaps the best example of the transition from log to stone construction is found in Herr House near Lancaster (see page 36). Its shape, like its predecessor's, is rectangular and has a sharply slanting roof and no dormers; but it does have a typical central chimney. It may originally have had a thatched roof, in common with the log houses, but if it did, this was replaced a long time ago by shingles. Although the house is two and a half storeys high, the light for the upper floors is supplied only by the relatively small windows in the gable ends. The sharp angles of the roof and the absence of dormers closely resembles that of the Sisters' House at Ephrata. The Moravian buildings at Bethlehem also have similar roofs, but the upper storeys are lighted by flat-topped dormer windows. Later in the 18th Century, a bigger and more elaborate stone house was built, of which "The House of the Miller" at Millbach (in Lebanon County) is an excellent example (see page 36). This type of house was the cherished dream of the immigrant, and all the native skill and artistry possible in that day were spent upon its design and construction. In this particular house, the great walnut chairs stood by the fireplace over which hung a Kentucky rifle; the long stretcher or sawbuck table was placed in the center of the dining hall, while the open cupboards against the walls held the family pewter and tableware. The floors of this type of house were built of oak of random size. The doors, in two parts, had raised decorative panels and the familiar double-cock wrought iron hinges. The ceilings were supported by massive beams while the windows were deeply set in plain, undecorated walls. The simple lines of the furniture completed the severe setting which was not unlike the houses of Germany that the immigrants had left behind.

While Herr House and the Millbach House are interesting, they are not typical of the thousands of farm houses of Southeastern Pennsylvania, for they were greatly influenced by the combined house-and-barn structure of Upper Bavaria. More typical was the farm house with a separate barn. Most of these houses were built of stone or brick with a chimney in the middle of each gable end. In addition to the Anglicized style of the chimney, the roof had less pitch and sometimes had dormer windows. Later, the house was greatly enlarged and instead of being rectangular in shape, it was either L- or T-shaped. Occasionally, eaves were carried across the gable ends of the house, thus providing a watershed around the entire house.

It was not long before the aggressive Carpenter's Company in Philadelphia, the importation of English architectural books and the subsequent manufacturing of mill work in Philadelphia, combined to bring the Georgian influence to the backwoods of Pennsylvania. The struggle continued between the German craftsmen and those who used English materials, until finally the latter won. Houses, churches, and public buildings of the Georgian style became the vogue in areas thickly populated with people of German heritage. York, Lebanon, Lehigh, Berks and Lancaster Counties appear more English today than German, but many of the inhabitants can "sell you" in Pennsylvania Dutch.

Many of the early houses of the Pennsylvania Dutch region were supplemented by a small building known as the summer house. These houses were often as large as the log houses of the original settlers and resembled them closely. In them, bake ovens were built at the back of the huge fireplaces, with an iron door to protect them from the fire itself. Before baking, the oven was charged with live coals from the hearth and these were allowed to remain in the oven until the walls had absorbed enough heat to bake bread or pies, after which the coals were scraped back into the fireplace. Sometimes this summer kitchen was built as part of the main house, and in such cases, it occupied much of the ground floor. Here the farmer's family worked and lived in the summer, the remainder of the house being used only at night, when all retired to their rope beds, chaff filled mattresses and linen sheets. In the winter, the family moved to the first floor of the house so that constant heat of the large fire would reduce the chilliness of the bedrooms overhead. In contrast to the problems of heating the house was the necessity for a cold storage space for such typical farm products as apples, turnips, celery, and potatoes, not to mention cheese and smoked meats. In later houses, an arched cooling cellar was an adjunct to the regular cellar. It usually extended beyond the foundation of the house and had a small chimney-like opening that permitted ventilation. Sometimes these excavations, made in the yard, are still to be recognized by a small mound with a well bolted door.

The early barns of the Pennsylvania Dutch were often built against a hill so that the ground floor was exposed on one side, the two ends half concealed with ground, and the remaining side completely banked with ground. On the back or banked side of the barn, huge doors permitted the entrance of teams pulling tall loads of hay or wheat. This area was known as the main barn floor, where grain was threshed in the summer, and equipment stored in the cold winter. On each side of the main floor were lofts for the storing of hay and straw for winter use. The lower level of the barn was occupied by stables and feeding entries. The doors and windows to these areas were protected by a wooden canopy which projected five to ten feet beyond the main structure of the barn. The lower level, protected by the ground on three sides, was warm and comfortable in the winter for horses and cattle. Considering the barn to be of equal importance to the house, the farmer spared nothing in quality of material or workmanship. The fitted and pinned joints of these old barns obviously served them well, for many are intact and unusually sound today.

Some of the best existing evidences of early rural economy are the large mills that dot the countryside. Most often they were built of stone with beautifully proportioned windows and doors. At the gable end, a hoist lifted the bags to the doors that opened from each floor. The first floor level was usually higher than the ground and the entrance was reached by walking up a few steps. Both the entrance and the steps were usually protected by a small triangular-shaped canopy similar to the canopies that are to be found on early barns. Water power was supplied by a mill race, diverted from a stream by a dam, and the grain was ground by the turning millstones. The writer can well remember taking roasted corn to the mill to be ground, from which the miller removed a portion for his pay. Ground corn was a basic ingredient of food for the Pennsylvania Dutch, and from it was made the well-known "mush and milk" for the evening meal. The excess was fried the next morning and served with syrup or ground meat.

FURNITURE

Rarely does one find a piece of Pennsylvania Dutch furniture truly representative of the early period, but once in a while a country auction still produces a candle stand, a wooden trammel, an open cupboard or a sawbuck table with its bench. The candle stands have bases of roughly hewn timber, the cupboards have plain doors and iron hinges, while the sawbuck tables have straight, undecorated edges with a wedge through the stretcher to hold it together. Long benches were placed at the table for eating and later moved to the wall, or else they were set before the fireplace for resting or working. These pieces were comparatively rare, even when they were the custom, and their subsequent common destruction for a more fashionable article has made them practically non-existent today.

Much of the furniture that is associated with the early years of colonization was, of course, copied from European prototypes. The plank seat chair, the sawbuck table, the open cupboard, the walnut armchair, and the painted chests, all bear a marked similarity to the 17th Century furniture of the German and Swiss peasant.

The plank seat chair, with its splayed legs and shaped back, is sometimes called the Moravian chair, a higher one being designed for the brother, and a lower one for the sister. The plank seat was reinforced with two pieces of wood which were inserted crosswise, in dovetail fashion, to give strength to the chair seat and to provide a better setting for the legs. The massive armchairs were made with simply turned front legs, solid backs, or with shaped splats, solid seats, and rectangular shaped rungs. The edges of the rungs, particularly in the front, were often rounded as the result of constant wear. The sawbuck table was also popular, for it was not only easy to make but it was sturdy and practical. Some were made of pine, others, usually more elaborate, were made of walnut. The delicacy of the turnings of many of these tables shows the influence of styles found in other areas of the colonies. Some rare pieces have the regular stretcher with a horizontal one mounted on top. Probably this was done to reinforce the vertical stretcher against the steady wear of the farmers' shoes, which more often than not must have rested upon it.

The open cupboards were also made of native woods. The top was usually decorated by a cornice which varied in size and detail, according to the design of the cupboard. Two or three shelves were placed in the upper section with plate rails, and usually one shelf had a row of triangular shaped cut-outs along the edge to hold pewter spoons. The lower shelves were concealed by a plain, unpanelled door. Later, a raised panel was introduced into the door, and the shelf storage space was supplemented by various arrangements of drawers. Some cupboards did not have feet, while others were supported by straight pieces of heavy timber placed near the ends and perpendicular to the main axis of the cupboard. Supports such as these are also to be found on early chests.

The beautifully decorated Pennsylvania Dutch chest, designed differently in separate counties, is particularly well-known and many good examples are illustrated in this book. In his publication, "The Furniture of the Pilgrim Century," Wallace Nutting states that the chest was the first piece of furniture known to man. Not only did it serve as a storage place for his treasures, but also as a bench by day and a bed by night. The earliest chests that were made are rare in Pennsylvania, but in the second half of the 18th Century they were abundantly produced and many examples of them can be seen today. Probably the rarest chest is the unpainted, architectural type. The front of this was divided into three sections by fluted columns, joined near the top by an arched band which stretched across the entire length. The sunken panels were not decorated, but on the top band are sometimes found dates, initials, hearts or tulips inlaid in white to contrast with the walnut wood of which these chests were most frequently made. In Lancaster County, chests of similar decoration and architectural construction were sometimes made of soft wood. The columns were generally painted in two colors, the sunken panels carrying a light color as a background for tulips or other motifs. Lebanon County chests have more boldly painted tulips and these are enclosed in a panel formed by simulated balusters. Montgomery and Lehigh Counties are best known for their geometric chest designs, while Berks County is associated with the unicorn design and Dauphin County with the floral patterns of the Ranks and of John Selzer. The lovely blue and green backgrounds and the brilliant colors of the flowers on this type of chest fully display the folk artists' inherent love for pattern and color. In Europe, it was the custom for the groom to give chests such as these to the bride, and, in addition, beds, chairs and cupboards. In America, the "dower chest" was the father's gift to his daughter to enable her to accumulate linens and other necessities to start her home when she married. Also given to the bride for her more delicate finery was the small oval bride's box which was decorated with flowers or figures.

Considerably rarer than the painted chest and the bride's box are decorated cupboards, wardrobes, grandfather clocks, chests of drawers and salt boxes. Many are so similar to their European cousins that the identifying feature of the Pennsylvania pieces is not so much their decorative motif as it is the native woods of which they are made. Although painted furniture was made in other parts of America, it was not as popular anywhere as it was in Pennsylvania.

POTTERY

Today, museums and publications have done much to revive the interest in early American pottery, with the result that many craftsmen and manufacturers are adapting old motifs to modern styles. The designs of the Pennsylvania Dutch potters figure largely in this movement and close reproductions of some have been made.

The natural red clay of Pennsylvania and the imported white slip were used by the early craftsmen for their slip and sgraffito ware. The potter would first remove the top soil of the earth and dig up his clay, then take it to his shop where he ground and diluted it with water until it formed a thick uniform mass. It was then stacked where it would not freeze, but would remain moist until ready to use. The life of a potter was not without anxieties and disappointments, despite the obvious pleasure attending creative work of this kind. Throwing pieces on the wheel was (and is) a difficult but fascinating skill. After molding, the pieces were set out to dry. Later, they were placed in a kiln which was sealed so that each piece would be evenly heated and the fumes could only escape through the top vent. After thirty to fifty hours of firing, which might use as much as three cords of wood, the kiln was left to cool for a week. Then, with mixed emotion, the potter removed his ware. Some pieces were perfect, some had curious and unforseen shapes and colors while others were complete failures that had to be discarded.

It is reasonable to suppose that many experienced potters came from Europe at the beginning of the 18th Century when the making of pottery (and the use of the tulip motif) had reached its height in the Palatinate Valley. As many as thirty potters are known to have worked in Bucks County alone and there existed in one area seven potteries hardly more than two miles apart.

Due to the natural limitation of wood and the rigid control of pewter by the English guilds, much of the kitchenware was made of pottery. One of the most important of such pieces was the pie plate in which they would bake their favorite American berry and fruit pies. Decorated pottery of the Pennsylvania Dutch is known as polychrome, slip, and sgraffito ware, all of which are sometimes classified under the general heading of tulip ware. All types were made of the native red clay, but a different technique was used in their decoration. The slip ware, for instance, was decorated by holding a small slip cup in the hand and, after tilting it so that the slip could flow out of the quills, it was moved across the flat surface of the plate. These slip cups had from two to seven openings in which quills were placed for an even control of the slip. The transition from a number of even lines to one line was affected by turning the quills round, so that the slip from all the quills fell on one line. For outlining, lettering and dating, either a special cup was used that had one quill, or else all but one of the quills were closed on the regular cup. After the slip had dried sufficiently so that it would not smear, the flat clay was beaten or rolled until the slip was forced into it and the clay was even again. At this stage, the clay was about half dry and was ready to be placed on a convex form and pressed into its final shape. After this, it was trimmed and the edge serrated by a small coggle wheel. The piece was then allowed to dry completely and finally was glazed and fired.

The making of the sgraffito ware was very similar to the slip, except for the method of decoration. After the clay was half dry, it was shaped and the concave side was covered with white slip. Later, areas of the white slip were removed with a sharp stick so that the red clay underneath appeared, forming the design or pattern of slip super-imposed on red clay. The border inscriptions were also scratched at this time so that when the piece was dry it could be glazed and fired.

Only a few hundred pieces of sgraffito ware are known to exist today. This is due to the fact that they were mostly made for gifts or presentation pieces. The white slip was rare and costly; furthermore such pieces required more than the average potter's skill to create. Although some experts believe that all sgraffito ware was made by highly skilled potters, other disagree and point to the uniformity of the products of one pottery. It seems unlikely, however, that an itinerant would make peacocks for George Hubener and for no one else. We can suppose, therefore, that Hubener himself executed his own peacock motif with all of its variations.

Still rarer than sgraffito ware is the polychrome pottery, decorated in many colors. This decoration was used quite extensively in Switzerland and to a lesser extent in Germany. The pottery could be made by either the slip or sgraffito technique. As it was made of many colors, such as red, green, yellow, white and black, only the most experienced craftsmen were able to create it successfully. The colored slips were very expensive, which is another reason why so comparatively few pieces were made.

Although slip and sgraffito pottery were occasionally used for practical purposes, it was usually the common red clay from which household pieces like mixing bowls, pitchers, jugs, crocks, measures and pie plates were made. These undecorated pieces were soon manufactured in large quantities, but were so eagerly sought in the early days that sometimes before the kiln opened, crowds gathered to make certain of getting the piece they needed. Besides the more familiar deep vegetable or meat dishes, plates and oval platters, other pottery objects were made, such as betty lamps and betty lamp holders, toys and roofing tiles. These tiles were rectangular in shape, measuring about five by thirteen inches. The upper side was concave so that the water flowed toward the center. A lug, or knob, was molded on the bottom of the tile for securing it to the roof. A few of these old tile roofs still exist in the Oley Valley area.

The most prized pieces of Pennsylvania Dutch pottery today are undoubtedly the decorated deep dishes, pie plates and oval platters. On them are to be found delightful patterns incorporating the familar motifs of the dove, deer, horse, rabbit, fish, eagle, pomegranate, tulip, fuchsia, olive leaf, forget-me-not, and the lily-of-the-valley. Colonial troopers on horseback were a favorite subject of David Spinner who is also famous for his "Lady Okle" plate and his deer's chase pattern. Johannes Neesz also favored the Colonial trooper motif and frequently added an inscription. George Hubener is famous for his double dove plates, also for his peacock motif with a double line inscription round the edge. Some of the other potters were not so prolific but we find many unusual pieces such as the fan-shaped flower vase by Charles Headman and the oval fluted sgraffito plate by Samuel Troxel. John Nase was also a well-known potter of this time and several of his pieces appear in the illustrated section of this book.

HENRY WILLIAM STIEGEL AND HIS GLASS

Heinrich Wilhelm Stiegel was not a craftsman, and none of his biographers credit him with having blown a single piece of glass. Despite this fact, the finest American glass of the late 18th Century has come to be known as Stiegel Glass. The beautifully colored, expertly etched, engraved, pressed and enamelled glass associated with his name was made under his direction by skilled blowers imported from Switzerland, Germany, England, Italy and Holland. Equal in quality to some of the best glass imported from Europe, Stiegel Glass is unquestionably one of the finest contributions to the crafts of early America, although the direct connection with European craftsmanship must not be overlooked in its evaluation. To the Rago brothers of Venice, for instance, is attributed the diamond and daisy-in-the-square patterns frequently found on Stiegel Glass. Credit is usually given to German craftsmen for unmolded glass pieces, to the English for wine glasses and to the Swiss for the rare enamelled pieces so cherished by collectors today. Typical designs on colored enamel glass, samples of which are illustrated in this book, are the rooster and parrot; also architectural motifs and various birds and animals surrounded by foliage or flowers.

Illustrations of Pennsylvania Dutch glass are acknowledged as Stiegel *type* glass. The qualification is necessary, for many pieces that are loosely credited to Stiegel were made elsewhere at a later period, possibly by Stiegel employees or imitators. For this reason, few authorities, if any, will guarantee a piece of early glass as definitely of Stiegel origin, although unquestionably some of the pieces in this book must have been made at his works. Stiegel's ledgers indicate the style in which he specialized—domed and footed urns, cream jugs, bottles and pitchers, mugs, vases, jiggers, decanters and cruet designs. These pieces were sold as far afield as Boston and Baltimore, not to mention New York where Stiegel is known to have had a shop of his own. Besides the white transparent flint glass, typical colored pieces were blown in amethyst, amber, green and blue.

Stiegel was born in Cologne on May 13, 1729. There is no documentary evidence of his legal right to the title of Baron and it is therefore assumed to have been affectionately bestowed upon him by his friends at Manheim, Pennsylvania. The fact that Stiegel's father died at an early age may have had some influence on the emigration of the family to the New World. Accompanying his mother and brother, Anthony, he arrived in Philadelphia on August 3, 1750, and very little is known of his travels until in 1752 he was employed by Jacob Huber at Elizabeth Furnace in Lancaster County. In less than a year, he married Huber's daughter and by 1756, together with the Stedmans of Philadelphia, he owned and operated Elizabeth Furnace. In four years, Stiegel became a naturalized citizen and changed his name from Heinrich Wilhelm to Henry William. This latter change is recorded on some stove plates that were later cast at Elizabeth Furnace. It was at Elizabeth Furnace that Stiegel first built a glass furnace. The new experiments in glass blowing proved highly successful, and he embarked for England to study the modern method employed in that country and also to bring back blowers to work for him in Pennsylvania. The demand for window glass, bottles and other products steadily rose and soon the number of men in his employ rose from ten to one hundred and thirty. During this most successful period of his life,

Stiegel imported bricks from England and built a luxurious mansion for himself at Manheim, the interior of which was equally elaborate. He lived and entertained lavishly and became a noted local benefactor of the church by presenting a tract of land for the erection of a German Lutheran Church at the nominal rental of "one red rose yearly hereafter."

Stiegel's good fortune, however, was not destined to last. Following the chaotic business conditions of 1772, he was forced to sell Channing Forge which, until that year, had operated very successfully in conjunction with Elizabeth Furnace. On May 5, 1774, recorded in his own handwriting is this sad epitaph to his ambitious career— "Glass House shut down." Reverses heaped one upon another in rapid succession until he ended up in a debtor's prison in Lancaster, only to be released by an act of the Pennsylvania legislature on December 24, 1774. Without his former business and stripped of all his possessions—his house with its beautiful furnishings, his horses, carriages, and hounds—he went back with his wife to Elizabeth Furnace, this time in the humble position of caretaker. He later moved into the parsonage of the Church at Brickerville where he earned a meager living by substituting for the school teacher who had gone to war. In the years 1781 and 1782, Stiegel's wife and mother died and on January 10, 1785, one day after receiving news of his brother's death, he himself died. It seems ironical that his body should lie in an unmarked grave, while his stove plates and famous handmade glass bear living witness to a dramatic life that had few equals in the early history of the Pennsylvania Dutch region.

METALWORK

Dependent upon shallow surface lodes that had been bared by erosion—similar to those used by the native Indians—the early colonists were able to make only small and very crude articles of metal. Slowly, this placer method of mining was replaced by shaft mining. However, it was not until Paul Revere evolved a method of rolling sheet metal, that the first real progress toward the development of metalwork in the New World was made. Thereafter, articles were no longer cast but were raised, spun or stamped. As a result, lighter and less cumbersome articles, as well as more ornate ones, were soon developed.

Deposits of iron ore were soon discovered in Pennsylvania and by 1727, the state was on its way to becoming an industrial iron center. Not only had it rich ore deposits, but it also had ample wood for fuel and limestone for flux. The first furnaces in the district produced pig iron, which was melted into molds to form pots, kettles, lamps and other household necessities. Although many of the early furnaces near Philadelphia were owned by Englishmen, they soon began, through popular demand, to cast the famous German stove plate. These plates were cast in open sand molds into which a pattern had previously been pressed. Unfortunately, these patterns which were expertly carved in low relief have all disappeared, except the one in the possession of the Bucks County Historical Society. The earliest stove was made of five plates. The remaining open end was inserted into the wall, the stove being charged from the adjoining room. The opening was usually in a fireplace which provided the only draft and outlet for the smoke. Later, the six plate stove was developed, it in turn being discarded for the ten plate stove which was used for baking as well as heating.

The local smith, in the true spirit of craftsmanship, not only supplied plain household necessities, but also decorated them in the finest European tradition. Common door hinges were sometimes shaped with cock's heads, tulips, butterfly wings, and stag horns. Latch finials were often tulip-shaped and the latch locks were decorated with small bevels and serifs. Ladle and skimmer handles were also designed with a similar degree of skill. There was little surface ornamentation on these early pieces, but occasionally a Conestoga wagon box has an intricate interlacing of patterns. Further examples of the blacksmith's craft are to be found in such objects as chandeliers, trammels, weathervanes, cranes for the fireplace, trivets, toasters, skewers and footscrapers.

Originally, the mother country expected the colonies to produce raw materials for the homeland, purchasing from her in return the finished manufactured product. This attitude was not long popular with the colonist whose aim of self-sufficiency in the various crafts was bolstered by the varied groups of craftsmen continually arriving from Europe. With iron ore flowing to American furnaces, clay to American potteries, and wool to American looms, the country became more and more independent in these industries. With pewter, however, the story was different. Tin, which is the largest constituent of pewter, was not abundant here and the English guilds restricted the export of pewter (made from the rich tin mines of Cornwall) to the finished articles already manufactured in England. Thus the American craftsman was confined merely to recasting old pieces that had originally been made abroad and, through long usage, were no longer serviceable. It therefore follows that very few American pieces of the 18th Century exist. It was not until the time of the American Revolution that Pennsylvania could boast of even two pewter craftsmen, namely William Will and Johann Christopher Heyne, about whom some mention should be made.

William Will was born in Germany but migrated to New York at an early age, and apprenticed himself to his brother who owned a shop in that city. Later, he opened a shop of his own in Philadelphia, but production was interrupted by the American Revolution (in which he served as a Colonel). Later, returning to pewtering, he achieved a high standard of craftsmanship with his coffeepots (the earliest ones known in America), tankards, mugs, plates, basins, spoons, ladles and, more particularly, with his famous Queen Anne teapots.

Johann Christopher Heyne was also born in Germany, and though his Lancaster products were influenced by English styles, some Teutonic design can be seen in most of his work. Two of his earliest pieces were the famous flagons of the Trinity Lutheran Church of Lancaster. These closely resemble German Guild tankards, with their flaring cylindrical bodies, feet of cherubs' heads, and their ball thumb pieces. Heyne is also well-known for his chalices, sugar bowls, whiskey flasks, plates, and one porringer. Also made in Pennsylvania were the so-called West Town and Kirk porringers but little appears to be known of their makers. The Kirk porringers were made in York, the touch marks reading "Elisha Kirk, Yorktown."

The tinware of the Pennsylvania Dutch (like the modern tin can) was not made entirely of tin, but of a sheet of iron which was rolled thin, cleaned in a pickling solution, and then dipped in a vat of molten tin. The thin coating of tin protected the sheet from rust. It also facilitated joining, for tin is much easier to solder than sheet iron. This manufacturing process was invented in England and a certain quantity of sheets of the so-called charcoal tin were evidently exported to the eager American tinsmiths. A few pieces were made before the revolution, but the industry did not gain its full height until the first half of the 19th Century. Household pieces were made principally in New England, Pennsylvania, and Ohio. The famous decorated pieces of the Pennsylvania Dutch were brightly painted or else were decoratively punched or pierced with the characteristic motifs. It is thought that most of the tinware was made by tinkers, though possibly some pieces were made by plumbers in their spare time. The most frequently found examples are coffeepots, cream pitchers, sugar bowls, measures, milk warmers, tea caddies, trinket boxes, tea kettles, trays, beakers and candle holders. The vessels were painted either red or black, or were sometimes japanned so that the texture of metal came through the semi-transparent finish. Over this, designs were painted, flowers being the most common, although examples of birds and fruit are occasionally found. The floral motifs were usually tulips, pomegranates or roses, while the birds were peacocks or pheasants, and the fruit—grapes, peaches or plums. In later years, a stencilling method of decorating was introduced which lacked the individuality of the former freehand method.

Unpainted tin generally was decorated by a method known as punching. The pieces were cut to shape and then a pattern embossed on the inside by softly striking a punch so that a depression was formed. A hole was not cut into the metal except on such articles as lanterns and foot warmers, where pierced openings permitted the heat or the light to escape. Still other tin pieces of utilitarian nature, such as hearth ovens, lamp fluid containers, children's bottles, measures, flasks, coffeepots, spice boxes, candle molds and betty lamps were not decorated at all.

Many copper and brass utensils were used by the Pennsylvania Dutch and we find warming pans with tulips and bird designs, finely wrought copper measures which were used by the distilleries in their retail trade, and sometimes even a marked brass or copper tea kettle. The attractively engraved patch boxes of the Kentucky rifles are another example of the use of brass. Practically nothing is known, however, of the early coppersmith in the Dutch country and it is probable that most of the copper and brass utensils that were used in early days came from abroad.

TEXTILES AND NEEDLEWORK

Flax was considered one of the essential crops on the early farm. The many refining processes through which it had to go before the threads could be woven into table-cloths and linens required the cooperation of both the male and female members of the family. Mary Meigs Atwater, in her book "The Shuttle Craft Book of American Hand Weaving," tells that "eight spinners were required to provide thread for one weaver, who could weave from one to eight yards in one day. As with many early enterprises, the entire family was involved, the children preparing bobbins and carding wool, the mother concerned with dyeing and weaving, and the father reputed to have occasionally flipped the shuttle and beat the weft."

A great impetus was given to weaving in Pennsylvania after the arrival of Francis Daniel Pastorius and his group of German weavers who settled in Germantown in 1683. The art became so popular and important in the district, that the flax blossom and the weavers' spool of thread were incorporated into the Germantown seal. Large flocks of sheep were raised at Germantown and in 1685, William Penn, who was always eager to maintain a sound economy in Pennsylvania, reported in England that the weaving industry was flourishing in his province, and that a good quality of cloth was being made.

Perhaps the best known and the most sought after product of the early loom was the woolen coverlet. Pennsylvania is particularly famous for the double woven, blue and white snowball and pine tree pattern. This coverlet required considerable skill in weaving, was striking in appearance, and doubtless was ample protection against the rigorous winters of the province. Variations occur in the coverlet, such as the doubling of the motifs, or the introduction of a lighter tint of blue which is pleasantly included in the pattern of the dark blue and the white.

Early in the 19th Century, the Jacquard loom was invented, and was soon introduced into America. This machine made so many new patterns and designs possible that the charming, geometric designs of earlier coverlets were rapidly forsaken for the newer and more fashionable covers. The first jacquard woven coverlets were made of homespun and home dyed yarn and many of them were soft and beautiful. The speed of the Jacquard loom, however, was soon matched by the mechanization of spinning, and the coverlet became just another manufactured product.

A great deal of linen was also woven in Pennsylvania and, as late as the present day, one frequently finds runners of old linen, as well as flax spinning wheels. After the locally grown flax had reached its maturity, it had to be retted, broken, and heckled before it could be used. The fibers were then combed straight and smooth and were spun into a thread on a flax wheel, operated by foot as the spinner sat near the wheel and manipulated the fiber with her hands.

Some color combinations occur in linen cloth, but blue squares or natural colored linen are most frequently found. Brown and yellow were sometimes used with blue, and a few rare pieces included green. Most of the linen, in its natural color, became softer and whiter after constant washing and ironing. This plain cloth was basic, and from it were made sheets and pillow cases, curtains, table covers, towels, samplers, men's shirts and nightshirts, ladies' dresses, and, of course, Conestoga wagon covers.

Most of the early samplers were made of linen (usually called homespun), and were of necessity narrow, for such was the capacity of the early looms. This, however, does not explain the narrow decorated towels of the Pennsylvania Dutch which were made a century and a half later—the shape must have been retained either through custom or choice. Many pieces were made by young girls for their dower chests, often displaying elaborate needlework for which they would have little time after they had assumed the responsibilities of a household. Some were embroidered with religious mottos, others with peacocks and other colorful birds, while yet others featured conventionalized flower motifs. These special towels are thought to have been for guests, or else used to cover the much used family towel.

When the household linen became so extensive that identification was necessary, the alphabet sampler gained in popularity. This provided the twelve year old girl with some experience in needlework before she undertook the making of samplers. On the rectangular shaped linen, moral precepts were most commonly embroidered by the child, and, if made in a school, the name of the teacher and the school were sometimes included. Buildings were commonly executed in naïve interpretations that often included birds nearly half the size of a house. The color of the thread was usually red, blue, green, gold, black or brown and the most popular technique was cross-stitch.

Of all the forms of colonial needlework, none is practised more today in rural Pennsylvania than the making of quilts. The social aspect is prominent in the making of friendship quilts, for here friends of the bride prepare patches of a specified size which she herself later sews together into a quilt. Most of the motifs are characteristic of the area and include baskets of flowers and fruits, eagles, cherry wreaths, acorns and birds.

The star motif is among the most popular for the over-all pattern, the stars being made up of many small diamond-shaped designs. Other patch motifs are called the Philadelphia pavement, log cabin, double Irish cabin, the spinning wheel, and the Star of the East.

A rare type of quilt is the one in which patches are skillfully sewn on top of a quilt in appliqué fashion. Conventionalized flower designs are very popular in this technique, while eagles and tulips are occasionally found.

CERTIFICATES AND MANUSCRIPTS

The so-called Fractur-Schrift (Fraktur-Schriften),* or manuscript illuminations and calligraphy of the Pennsylvania Dutch, made with quill pen, pencil and brush on paper, are divided into different groups. Three groups were directly connected with the schools of the area and are usually known as "Vorschrift" or specimens of handwriting (calligraphy), "Belohnung" or rewards of merit, and "Guldene A B C" or the primer. In the earliest schools, the Bible was the only textbook, and the problem of learning the alphabet was made more difficult by the fact that the child was simultaneously made to learn a Biblical quotation starting with the letter to be learned. Under the supervision of the teacher, the students wrote, or illuminated, the alphabet with homemade paints. Quite possibly these paints were made of a mixture of whiskey and a varnish composed of cherry tree gum diluted with water. Dr. Mercer, in "The Survival of the Mediaeval Art of Illuminative Writing Among the Pennsylvania Germans" describes a paint box discovered at the end of the 19th Century, in which bottles containing the residue of these ingredients were found in small compartments. Other primitive methods of mixing colors and inks were unquestionably copied from recipes in Germany, including tempera paint which was used on most of the book plates, probably with a good deal of improvisation.

The more important examples of Fractur-Schrift were undoubtedly made by teachers or professionals, although quite possibly designs were added in many instances by the family for whom the documents were created. The "Geburts-Schein" was a birth certificate, the "Tauf-Schein," a baptismal certificate, the "Trau-Schein," a wedding certificate, and the "Familien Register," the family register. These documents were not certificates in the true sense, for very few bore the signature of a public official, which would have given them legal significance.

In addition to the types already mentioned, there was the "Haus Segen," or house blessing, which very often included a prayer, the "Bucherzeichen" or book plate, indicating the name of the owner, the date of ownership, and sometimes the donor, and finally the "Lese-Zeichen," or bookmark.

Few examples of fractur are larger than fourteen by eighteen inches, although some larger ones are known to exist. For the most part, they are handsomely decorated with ornate letters and, besides floral, bird and fruit decorations, often include one or several of such typical motifs as the angel (usually with trumpet), mermaid, child, lamb, horse, deer, corn in ear, cross, crown, or the sun, moon and the stars. Like the tulip and the bird, the heart, symbolizing love or affection, was one of the most popular decorations introduced into the design. Some of the best illuminated pieces came from the Cloister at Ephrata, famous for the lily motif. One is not altogether surprised to find that their music sheets were often decorated in the same manner, for both music and drawing were regarded by Conrad Beissel (organizer of the Cloister) as evidences of "spiritual growth."

Fractur-Schrift, like all other Pennsylvania Dutch artistic expression, deteriorated during the Industrial Revolution. Printed copies appeared in the early part of the 19th Century, and little skill was required merely to enter a name on the certificate or to color in the angels. With this standardization of the various forms and motifs, all individuality and feeling of craftsmanship disappeared. A touching epitaph is to be found on the wall of the Bucks County Historical Society in the form of a small paint box once belonging to one of the early illuminators of the county.

* *The word "fractur," frequently spelled "fraktur," means to write in gothic characters at the same time as introducing a decoration or design in color.*

Above: Green Tree fire mark, made of cast lead and attached to a wooden shield. The sign indicated that the building on which it was fixed was insured by the Mutual Assurance Company, Philadelphia, 1784–1803. (Abby Aldrich Rockefeller Folk Art Collection)

Right: Outdoor oven and summer kitchen of whitewashed stone, belonging to the Reiff farm in the Oley Valley. The tiled roof is unusual. Below: The model of Penn Square, Reading, belonging to The Historical Society of Berks County, shows the architecture of the early days. The small building with the large sign, behind the market houses, was Conrad Weiser's trading store.

33

The clearance of forests simultaneously provided land for farming and wood for building. As there was no shortage of timber, the buildings were correspondingly lavish with this material. The log cabin made a satisfactory early dwelling.

These photographs, taken in the Dutch country, show the simple shapes and corner construction of the early cabin or house, which served many purposes. The residence in the winter landscape above was once a church.

The painting of design motifs on the walls of barns began in the early 19th Century. The barns on this page are also of about that date and are shown as they are today. The decorated barn below is at Wescoesville, Reading, in Lehigh County. (Photograph Courtesy The Historical Society of Berks County)

In the famous 18th Century Herr House, near Lancaster (Left), the high pitched roof and the absence of dormer windows suggest a Northern European influence.

Above: The exterior of the equally famous House of the Miller at Millbach, built in 1752, as it appears today. Interiors of this house appear later in the book. (Philadelphia Museum of Art)

Right: The realistically painted loon decoy, with glass eyes, originally used outdoors, was not merely the decorative object it is considered today. (Abby Aldrich Rockefeller Folk Art Collection)

Left: Pheasant weathervane for the roof of a house, cut out of sheet iron. Found at Monterey. (John D. Rockefeller III Collection)

Below: The well-known and beautiful Fisher House in the Oley Valley shows the influence of the 19th Century Georgian architecture that later became prevalent in the Dutch country.

Right: The Kauffman House in the Oley Valley is another example of 18th Century architecture which, with central chimney, is unlike the 19th Century Fisher House above. (Courtesy Bucks County Historical Society.)

Left: Lid, complete with hinges and hasp, from a Conestoga wagon tool box. This detail is indicative of the quality of workmanship throughout the wagon. (Philadelphia Museum of Art) Below: Iron hasp used in the tongue assembly of a Conestoga wagon. Signed "D Kumerle" by the craftsman. (Author's Collection) Bottom: Built to withstand hard usage and rough going, the covered wagon was named after the Conestoga Valley in Lancaster County. Such wagons were the principal vehicles for freight transport in the last half of the 18th Century. (Pennsylvania Farm Museum of Landis Valley)

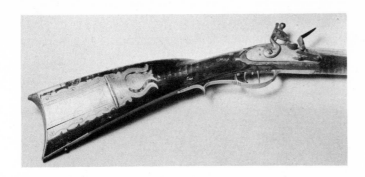

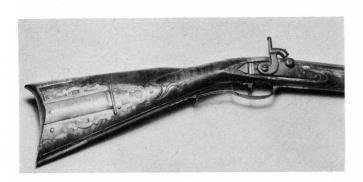

Pennsylvania craftsmen made few rifles with Pennsylvania Dutch motifs. Four such rare examples are illustrated on this page.

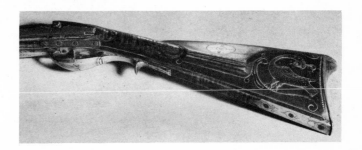

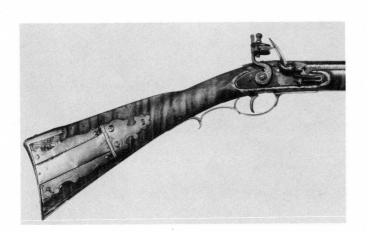

Above: Rifle with fowl carved on the butt. (McMurtrie Collection) Left: Rifle with daisy finial on the patch box. (Wilson Collection)

I N D O O R S

As we enter the early house through the front door we find either a hall or a room which had to serve many purposes—frequently the kitchen. The old door itself was usually of interesting design, with panelling and broad hinges. Above: Corner of a room with entrance door in the House of the Miller at Millbach. (Restored in the Philadelphia Museum of Art)   See pages 63 and 99 for detail photographs of the corner cupboard and sawbuck table. Left: Painted and decorated child's bench. (The Metropolitan Museum of Art. Gift of Mrs. Robert W. de Forest, 1933)

Below: Entrance hall in the House of the Miller at Millbach. Note the two piece door, the framed needlework on the wall, the peasant chair, and the oak beamed ceiling. (Philadelphia Museum of Art)

Below: Iron door hinges of the early 18th Century—similar to the ones at the top of the opposite page.

Left: In the Kauffman
House in the Oley Val-
ley (Exterior, Page 37)
is this simple, yet typical
fireplace with panelled
wood. (Courtesy Bucks
County Historical So-
ciety.)
Below: Primitive can-
dle stand with bird's nest
type top, made to rotate.

Below: Typical tulip and heart motifs of the
Pennsylvania Dutch are incorporated into the de-
sign of this iron stove plate cast by Stiegel at
Elizabeth Furnace, Lancaster County, about 1760.
(Philadelphia Museum of Art)

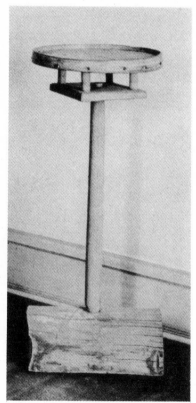

Above: Stove plate of Cain about to slay Abel. Note the Romanesque setting. Dated 1741. (Philadelphia Museum of Art)   Below: Furnished room in the Philadelphia Museum of Art with the appurtenances usually found in a kitchen. The decorated cupboard with glass doors on the top is commonly known as a Dutch cupboard. (Photograph by A. J. Wyatt, Staff Photographer)

Above: Stylized rooster carved in pine wood and polychromed. Found in New York. (Abby Aldrich Rockefeller Folk Art Collection) Left and Below: Ladderback chair and splat back armchair. (The Metropolitan Museum of Art. Gift of Mrs. Robert W. de Forest, 1933)

44

Left: Polychrome figures carved of wood. The dog is attributed to Mounts, the other two to Shimmel. (Author's Collection)

Right: The decorative motifs on this box are very unusual, and the green background color is unique. The function of the box is not known. (Author's Collection)

Below: Cast iron stove made about 1823 by District Furnace in Berks County.

One is never in a house very long before one detects either the absence or presence of children. Seldom were they painted more attractively than this "Girl on Balcony" made between 1840 and 1850. This canvas may have come from the Shenandoah Valley and is commonly credited as being of Pennsylvania Dutch origin. Found at Bethlehem. (Abby Aldrich Rockefeller Folk Art Collection)

Below: Painted cast iron rabbits, probably used as lawn ornaments. (Abby Aldrich Rockefeller Folk Art Collection)

Below: Decorated bent wood trinket box. (Metropolitan Museum of Art. Gift of Mrs. Robert W. de Forest, 1933)

46

Above Left: Decorated trinket box of bent wood. (The Metropolitan Museum of Art. Gift of Mrs. Robert W. de Forest, 1933)   Above Right: Bride's box. The representation of a colonial horseman on this type of box is very rare. Found near Landsdale.   Below: Interior with authentic Pennsylvania Dutch pieces. Note the double door with "H" and "L" hinges and original latch.

Right: Salt glaze earthenware moneybank made by R. C. Remmey in the late 19th Century. (Philadelphia Museum of Art. Photograph by A. J. Wyatt, Staff Photographer)

Below: Seated woman of polychromed wood. Found near Ephrata. (Abby Aldrich Rockefeller Folk Art Collection)

Bottom Right: Sugar bucket and lid, with painted decoration of bands, known as Lehn ware. (The Metropolitan Museum of Art. Gift of Mrs. Robert W. de Forest, 1933)

Above: "Jean Mac-Donald Lee Myers." Although found in New York, this painting is generally regarded as of Pennsylvania Dutch origin. c. 1840. (Abby Aldrich Rockefeller Folk Art Collection) Left: Candle box with unusual fruit motif. (The Metropolitan Museum of Art. Gift of Mrs. Robert W. de Forest, 1933)

Left: Pottery bird whistle made by John Nase, 18th Century. (Philadelphia Museum of Art)
Center: Early 19th Century birth certificate, interestingly found in Piqua, Ohio, where the Dutch tradition strayed. (Columbus Gallery of Fine Arts)
Bottom Left: Powder horn engraved with typical Pennsylvania Dutch motifs. The tulip and the head of the unicorn are very evident. (Author's Collection)
Bottom Right: Child's walnut chair of the 19th Century. (Philadelphia Museum of Art)

Above Left: Child's high chair. (Mr. and Mrs. Samuel Dyke Collection)   Above Right: Painted bird ornament with glass eye.   Below Left: Chalkware dog ornament found in Lancaster County.   (John D. Rockefeller III Collection)   Below Right: An example of fractur with elaborate letters.

Two pages of children's rocking horses, chairs, and a miniature cradle. The delightful horse above is in the Pennsylvania Farm Museum of Landis Valley. The toy cradle below, only one foot long, complete with patchwork quilt, is in Mrs. Roy Brenneman's Collection.

The chair at the left, designed for a child, is brightly painted, and belongs to Mrs. Lee Boyer, while the wooden rocking horse at the bottom is from the Philadelphia Museum of Art. All the pieces on these pages are probably 19th Century.

Three more items for the child. Above: Toy horse of painted wood, found in Carlisle. Left: Surrey with wooden wheels. (Miss Esther Lenhardt Collection) Below: Wagon with "real" underfittings.

*Above: Corner of a room furnished with
authentic Pennsylvania Dutch pieces. Left:
Three-legged wooden stool. Below: Poplar
wagon seat with a cutout heart design. c. 1780.
Seats such as this were placed at the front of a
wagon or cart for driver and passengers. (The
Metropolitan Museum of Art. Gift of Mrs.
Robert W. de Forest, 1933)*

Above Left: Early candle stand with hand cut threaded stem and unusually heavy base.   Above Center: Continental soldier iron doorstop. (Abby Aldrich Rockefeller Folk Art Collection) Above Right: Poplar corner shelves, one of which is cut as a spoon rack. c. 1750. (The Metropolitan Museum of Art. Gift of Mrs. Robert W. de Forest, 1933)   Below: Birth certificate decorated with borders of flowers, birds, and hearts.

On these pages are some fine examples of fractur technique (Fractur-Schrift). This is a combination of quill drawing and washes of color. The art was employed for religious as well as secular purposes, and is most commonly found on baptismal, marriage, and wedding certificates. Above: An example of late 18th Century fractur. (In The Brooklyn Museum Collection)   Below: Illuminated oblong pages, taken from a book. (In The Brooklyn Museum Collection)

Above Right: Steel pen drawing in sepia, found in Vermont but probably of Pennsylvania Dutch origin. (Paul Mellon Collection, Courtesy Downtown Gallery)

Above Left and Center: Two ornamental book plates.

Below: Boxes painted black with red and white flowers like this one are known as Bucher Boxes. Bucher is thought to have worked near Adamstown, Pennsylvania. (Author's Collection)

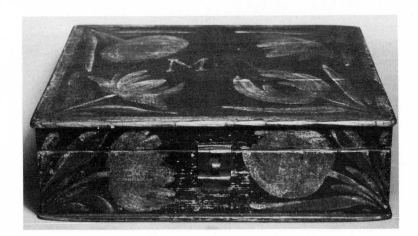

On these pages are various objects with "pairs of birds"—a theme which was always popular in Pennsylvania Dutch folk art.

Above: Ornamental certificate from the Bucks County Historical Society.

Left: Chest of drawers, decorated with a conventional design. c. 1834. Note that the design is slightly different on each drawer. (Philadelphia Museum of Art)

Pair of pottery ornaments. This hen and rooster are in polychrome finish and were made by John Nase. 18th Century. (Philadelphia Museum of Art)

Below: Birth Certificate with two pairs of ornamental birds.

Right: Fractur by Heinrich Otto, consisting of pairs of peacocks and parrots. Lancaster County, 1792. (Philadelphia Museum of Art. Photograph by A. J. Wyatt, Staff Photographer)

Left: Carved wood, poly-chromed eagle by Schimmel. Found in Carlisle. (Abby Aldrich Rockefeller Folk Art Collection)

Below Left: Collection of chalkware displayed in a decorative corner cupboard. See page 64 for a close-up view of the chalkware.

Opposite Page, Center Right: Polychromed wooden bust of George Washington, found in Wilmington, Delaware, but considered of Pennsylvania origin. (Abby Aldrich Rockefeller Folk Art Collection)

Opposite Page, Bottom: Lion ornament in pottery by John Nase, early 19th Century. (Philadelphia Museum of Art)

Right: An unusually fine hanging corner cupboard from the Millbach House. (Philadelphia Museum of Art)

Left: A close-up view of the slip ware jar in the cupboard above, decorated with two cocks, and tulip design. Dated 1787. (Philadelphia Museum of Art)

View of the corner cupboard reproduced on page 62, showing in some detail the interesting group of brightly painted chalkware figures.

A splendid example of chalkware ornament is this attractive stag, found in Bucks County in 1883.
(John D. Rockefeller III Collection)

Above: An unusual slip ware bulb kettle, found in Montgomery County. c. 1830. (Philadelphia Museum of Art)

Right: Sgraffito ware flowerpot with inscription. c. 1826. (Philadelphia Museum of Art)

Right: Puzzle jug made by Philip Kline, about 1809. The side displays the national emblem in a boldly scratched outline proclaiming "Liberty".

Below: Flowerpot with interesting moldings and floral and bird decoration. Round the rim is an inscription indicating the maker (Samuel Troxel) and the purchaser of the piece. Both these examples are in the Philadelphia Museum of Art.

Left: Wooden reel used in the making of textiles in the 18th Century. (Philadelphia Museum of Art) Center: Interior of the Cloister of Ephrata, showing spinning wheels, carding bench, and other textile machinery used when the colony flourished. Notice the half-timbered construction of the room. Below Left: Jacquard woven coverlet dated 1847, in dark blue and white. (Mrs. Roy Brenneman Collection) Below Right: Wool and cotton coverlet, dated 1835, also woven on the Jacquard loom. (Philadelphia Museum of Art)

Top Left: Jacquard woven linen and wool coverlet with bird and flower motif, dated 1839. (Philadelphia Museum of Art) Top Right: Jacquard woven coverlet with white background, and pattern in red and blue. (Author's Collection) Center: Another interior view of the Cloister at Ephrata, containing loom, reel, and shuttle. Right: Unusually high seated chair with perfect finials on both front and back legs. This was sometimes called a spinning chair.

Two pages of excellent examples of Stiegel type glass. Above are engraved decorations on white flint glass. From left to right: covered flip jar, tumbler with diamond shaped diapering, and a small jigger. (Edward L. White Collection) Below: Three drinking glasses with polychrome enamel decoration, representing the steeple design, a dog chasing a hare, and a bird amongst foliage. (Edward L. White Collection)

Above: Additional examples of engraved white flint glass, including covered mug and flip jar (Charles C. Wolfe Collection), and tumbler (center) in Miss Theodora Herzmann's collection.

Below: Tumbler with bull design and bottle with conventional birds and flowering plant, both in polychrome enamel. (Philadelphia Museum of Art)

Left: Kitchen interior of the Miller's House at Millbach. The curtains were printed by the blue and white resist method of the period. c. 1752. (Philadelphia Museum of Art. Photograph by A. J. Wyatt, Staff Photographer)

Above: Three examples of Stiegel type glass: Birds and foliage in polychrome enamel on jigger, white flint glass flip tumbler with diamond pattern and fluted base, also typical example of salt cellar design.

Right: Stiegel type glass creamer in white flint.

Left: Large Stiegel type sapphire blue sugar bowl and cover in expanded diamond design. (In The Brooklyn Museum Collection)

Below: Corner of the dining room of Dr. B. N. Osburn's residence, showing typical simply designed cupboard. Note the rack for the spoon display, also the coffee grinder at the right.

English pewter charger with fractur motif engraved on the back. This example is probably unique. (Courtesy, Henry Francis du Pont Winterthur Museum)

Above Left: Decorated Dutch cupboard, filled with china and decorative objects. The chair is a fine example of ladderback design. Above Right: Stiegel type glass mug, with colorful parrot on a green branch. Bottom Row: Stiegel type glass mug with rooster design, glass jigger with an architectural motif, and bottle with a white bird in a foliated circle, all in polychrome enamel.

Right: Fruit bowl, in amber colored Stiegel type glass. (Philadelphia Museum of Art)

Below: Blue flint Stiegel type glass creamer.

Bottom Left: Stiegel type white flip glass with fluted base, and engraved floral decoration around the top.

Bottom Right: Corner cupboard, carved with the name of Caleb Pusey, and dated 1717. (Philadelphia Museum of Art)

Two attractive drinking mugs of sgraffito ware. Above is a very fine specimen of 1801, and left, another one, made in 1816. Though quite different in style, both have typical floral designs including the popular tulip motif. (Philadelphia Museum of Art)

Right: Coffin-shaped tin tray with an amber crackle design in the center. (Author's Collection) Below Left and Right: Two typical trays of brightly painted tin. (Pennsylvania Farm Museum of Landis Valley) Bottom: Coffeepot and heater of painted tin, with japanned background, believed to have been made in the middle of the 19th Century.

Above: Tinware sugar bowl, coffeepot, and cream pitcher. The fact that virtually none of the motifs on Pennsylvania Dutch tinware "match" suggests that few sets, if any, were made. (Author's Collection)   Below: Decorative woodenware made by Lehn in Lancaster County in the 19th Century. All were formed on a lathe. (Author's Collection)

Right: Certificate with star and floral motifs in red, yellow, and blue. (Philadelphia Museum of Art, Titus C. Gesey Collection. Photograph by A. J. Wyatt, Staff Photographer) Below: Coffeepot with gooseneck spout, gold leaf on tin. Middle 19th Century.

Above: Two tin coffeepots, with gooseneck spouts and tulip designs in punched outline. (Philadelphia Museum of Art) Below: Early Moravian stretcher table. Note the unusual single key, serving for double stretcher.

Above: Three typical Pennsylvania Dutch objects of pewter. The basin was made by Love, the porringer is attributed to Elisha Kirk of Yorktown, and the bowl is similar to others signed Heyne. Below: Illuminated manuscript. (In The Brooklyn Museum Collection)

Slip ware pie dish with distelfink. (Philadelphia Museum of Art)

Left: Sgraffito ware pie dish. c. 1810. (Philadelphia Museum of Art)

Right: Sgraffito ware dish, with soldier on horseback.

Above: George Washing-
ton on horseback, shown
with trumpet and sword.
A sgraffito ware plate,
dated 1805. (Philadel-
phia Museum of Art)

Right: Another sgraffito
ware plate with military
theme. (The Metropoli-
tan Museum of Art.
Gift of Mrs. Robert
W. de Forest, 1933)

Above: Two ornate pie dishes (c. 1800) and a covered jar (c. 1830), all of sgraffito ware. (Philadelphia Museum of Art)

Below: "Light Dragoon" plate of sgraffito ware. This plate is arranged on the dresser on the opposite page. (The Metropolitan Museum of Art. Rogers Fund, 1913)

Opposite Page: Dresser of substantial proportions and restrained ornamentation. Found in the Mennonite country. (The Metropolitan Museum of Art. Rogers Fund, 1945)

The equestrian subject of these plates, like others on previous pages, will interest those who are able to remember the peculiar proportions of the "Officer's Charger," characterized briefly as having great weight in the forequarters, and a small head set upon a thickish neck. Its function was rather that of a battering ram than of an intelligent or sensitive animal.

While the "Officer's Charger" may or may not have been the inspiration of these designs, the proportions of the horse are at least reminiscent. The two plates on these pages are plainly marked as the work of David Spinner, one of the most famous "Pennsylvania Dutch" potters. They were made in glazed red earthenware, with decorations in sgraffito technique. c. 1800. (In The Brooklyn Museum Collection)

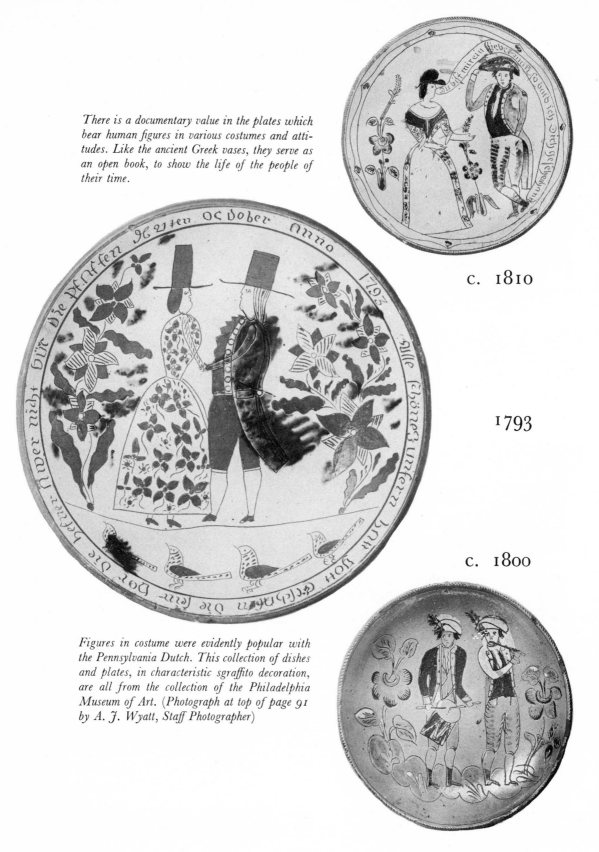

There is a documentary value in the plates which bear human figures in various costumes and attitudes. Like the ancient Greek vases, they serve as an open book, to show the life of the people of their time.

c. 1810

1793

c. 1800

Figures in costume were evidently popular with the Pennsylvania Dutch. This collection of dishes and plates, in characteristic sgraffito decoration, are all from the collection of the Philadelphia Museum of Art. (Photograph at top of page 91 by A. J. Wyatt, Staff Photographer)

Particularly famous are the two sgraffito plates reproduced in larger size on these pages. The one opposite (dated 1793) shows a couple in the dress of the period, and the one below (dated 1786) depicts English officers dancing with colonial dames to a tune played by the fiddler.

1800-1811

1786

1810

The plate immediately to the left has been identified as the work of David Spinner, the same craftsman who executed the examples on pages 88 and 89 and the "Deers Chase" on page 100.

1 8 2 6

1 8 2 3

1 7 9 3

Five more examples of pottery described generally as tulip ware, the first four of which are decorated in sgraffito technique, meaning that the decorations were scratched through the white slip covering the plate, before it was glazed. The last item (Right) is in slip ware, the design being directly applied over the earthenware base. The plate above is known to be the work of John Nase. (Philadelphia Museum of Art)

The two pieces on this page are also of sgraffito ware, with designs and inscriptions . The one above, representing the famous double-headed eagle motif, was made by George Hubener. Left: The plate with preening peacock and tulip design is unusual for the second circle of inscription; also generally accredited to George Hubener. (Philadelphia Museum of Art)

Above: Plate of glazed red earthenware with sgraffito decoration of double-headed eagle, heart, and two preening peacocks, made by George Hubener, Montgomery County. (Courtesy of The Brooklyn Museum. Lent by Mrs. George Burford Lorimer in Memory of George Burford Lorimer)

Below: Inlaid walnut chest of architectural design with simple flower and bird motif. (The Philadelphia Museum of Art, Titus C. Gesey Collection)

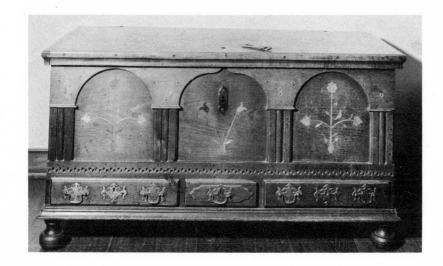

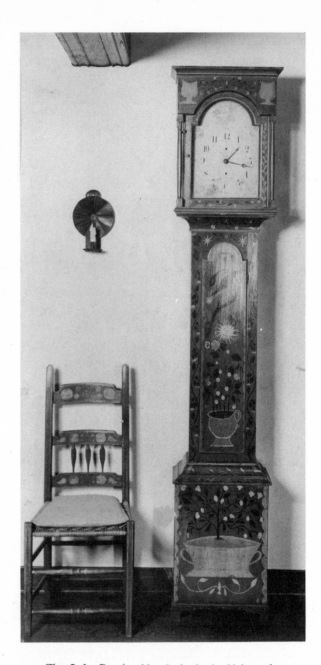

Top Left: Bench-table, the back of which can be swung over to form a table. Under the seat is a box for the family Bible. (Pennsylvania Farm Museum of Landis Valley) Left: A number of these round wooden boxes have been found in the Pennsylvania Dutch area. They were painted red and the stencil design was applied in blue. Their function is not known. (Author's Collection) Above: Decorated clock with birds, flowers, and urns painted on a pale red background. The chair is ornamented in a similar manner.

Left: A good example of the well-known Philadelphia comb back chair. This piece, of earlier origin than most, is believed to have been made about 1745.

Below: Dining room interior with Pennsylvania Dutch furniture, pottery, and linen. Note the grandfather clock in the corner, the fractur on the wall, and the upholstered armchair to the right.

Left: Slip ware dish with fish design and inscription. (Philadelphia Museum of Art)

Bottom Left: Tin lantern with punched motif on the lid. The openings are decorative and provide a supply of oxygen for the burning candle. (Author's Collection)

Bottom Right: Peasant chair with pierced back.

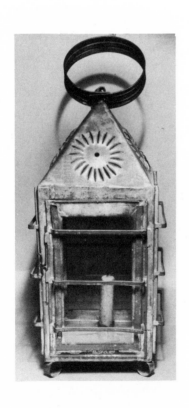

98

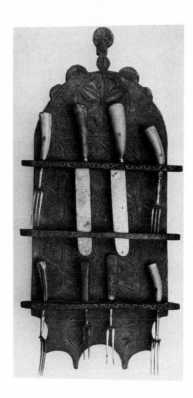

Above: Oval dish with sgraffito decoration and scalloped edge, by Samuel Troxel, dated 1823. (Philadelphia Museum of Art) Top Right: Knife and fork rack, complete with examples of early cutlery. (The Metropolitan Museum of Art. Gift of Mrs. Robert W. de Forest, 1933)

Below: Sawbuck table. c. 1750. (Philadelphia Museum of Art)

Above Left: Linen sampler with colored cross-stitch motifs. (Philadelphia Museum of Art)
Above Right: Sgraffito pie plate of a "Deers Chase" made by David Spinner. c. 1800. (Phila-
delphia Museum of Art)   Below: Room in the Philadelphia Museum of Art with furniture
and accessories of the 18th Century. The iron candle stand near the wainscot chair is probably
unique. (Photograph by A. J. Wyatt, Staff Photographer)

Above Left: Pewter flagon, made by Johann Christopher Heyne (1754–1780) in Lancaster County. The handle, lid, and thumb piece are of English design, while the remainder shows Teutonic influence. (In The Brooklyn Museum Collection) Above Right: Early pine corner cupboard with iron "H" hinges on both doors. Below: One of the oldest surviving American teapots, Queen Anne style, made by William Will (1764–1796) in Philadelphia. (In The Brooklyn Museum Collection)

Above: Kitchen setting in Washington's Headquarters at Valley Forge, showing traditional Pennsylvania Dutch architecture and furnishings.

Left: Molded and initialed slip ware dish, dated 1794. (Philadelphia Museum of Art)

Right: Stove plate of cast iron, made in 1749. (Philadelphia Museum of Art)

Below: The "Great Kas" in this photograph was probably made in Lancaster County. The white inlay tells that it was made for Georg Huber, Anno 1779. The table is known as a country Queen Anne type. (Philadelphia Museum of Art. Photograph by A. J. Wyatt, Staff Photographer)

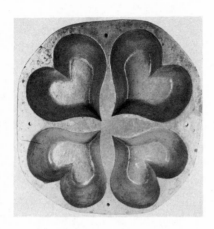

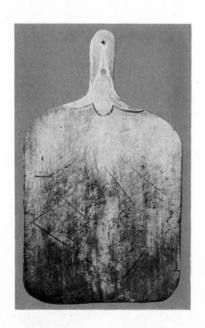

Above: Pottery cake mold of unusually large size ($12\frac{3}{4}''$ diameter × $2\frac{1}{4}''$ deep). Below: Wooden cutting board. (Pennsylvania Farm Museum of Landis Valley)

Above Right: Double trammel of wrought iron. 18th Century. (Philadelphia Museum of Art)

Left: Small decorated bucket, made by Lehn in Lancaster County. Initials are rarely found on any of his products. (Author's Collection)

Below: Red pottery bottle in the shape of a fish. A few spots of green slip were applied; one line is evident on the tail. (Rothschild Collection)

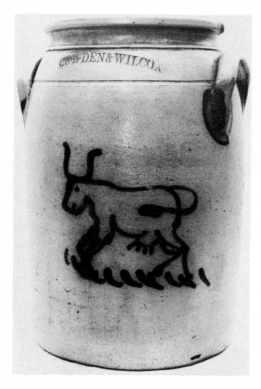

Top: Blown glass candle lamps, or lanterns, with metal bases and tops. Made between 1774 and 1810.   Above Left: Salt glazed earthenware jar with cow motif. (Pennsylvania Farm Museum of Landis Valley)   Above Right: Butter mold. (The Metropolitan Museum of Art. Gift of Mrs. Robert W. de Forest, 1933)

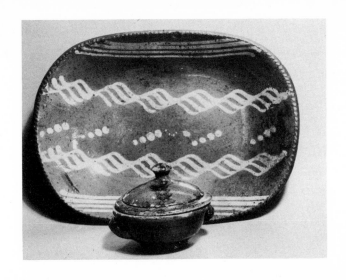

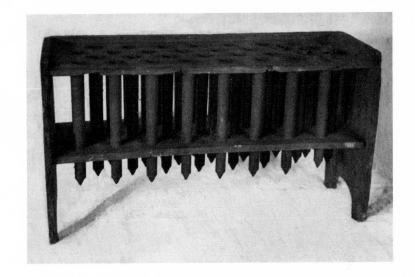

Above Left: Slip ware dish and small earthenware bowl with lid. (Author's Collection)
Above Right: Cookie mold, made of tin. (Philadelphia Museum of Art)
Center: Candle mold, made of tin and cherry wood. (Author's Collection)

Left: Earthenware betty lamp. (Pennsylvania Farm Museum of Landis Valley) Below: Long wooden bench. (The Metropolitan Museum of Art. Gift of Mrs. Robert W. de Forest, 1933)

Above: Kitchen fireplace in the Miller's house at Millbach (1752). Note, besides the fine display of pewter and cooking utensils, the Kentucky rifle at the left, commonly part of the kitchen scene. (Philadelphia Museum of Art) Below Left: The decoy duck may, along with the rifle, have been the means of getting many a bird into the cooking pot. (Abby Aldrich Rockefeller Folk Art Collection) Below Right: Tin coffeepot with gooseneck spout and punched motifs. This piece appears to have been made in the 18th Century, but many like it date from the middle of the 19th Century. (Author's Collection)

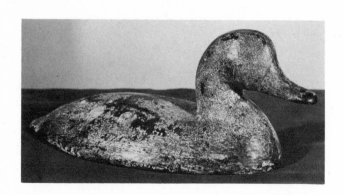

Above Left: Carved wooden salt box with unusual butterfly carving. (Pennsylvania Farm Museum of Landis Valley)   Above Right: Swan butter mold made of wood. (Pennsylvania Farm Museum of Landis Valley)   Below Left: Painted and decorated salt box, dated 1797.   Below Right: Base of copper warming pan with a typical bird motif. Probably of the 18th Century. (Author's Collection)

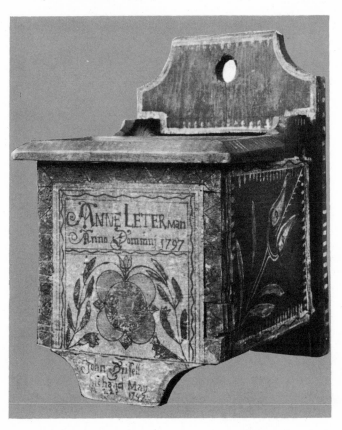

Above: Part of a Franklin stove plate, signed "Peter Grubb & George Ege." c. 1782. (Phila-delphia Museum of Art)   Below Left: Decorated board with handle and knob. (The Metropoli-tan Museum of Art. Gift of Mrs. Robert W. de Forest, 1933)   Below Right: Patch quilts.   The one at the left is in Mrs. Roy Brenneman's collection, the one at the right in the author's collection.

Opposite Page, Top: Bedroom from the House of the Miller at Millbach (1752). The decorative elements are boldly and simply executed in the traditional Pennsylvania Dutch manner. Reminiscent of Swedish work is the large table on the left with square turned legs, which should be compared with the ballusters on the stairway shown in the illustration on page 41. On the bedside table is the sgraffito ware mug illustrated on page 77, also a betty lamp. (Philadelphia Museum of Art)

Right: Small corner cupboard with painted decoration. (The Metropolitan Museum of Art. Gift of Mrs. Robert W. de Forest, 1933)

Below: Side table made of pine wood. (The Metropolitan Museum of Art. Gift of Mrs. Robert W. de Forest, 1933)

PEACOCK MOTIF

On these pages are various objects featuring the peacock motif, sometimes considered to represent the "eye of God."

Above: Two-handled sgraffito jar decorated in tones of deep yellow and green. On the reverse side is a tulip pattern (see page 114). Designed by George Hubener. Below Left: Woven coverlet with white ground, ornamented in red and tan with peacocks, houses, and flowers. (Mrs. Roy Brenneman Collection) Below Right: Kettle holder embroidered in crewel stitch.

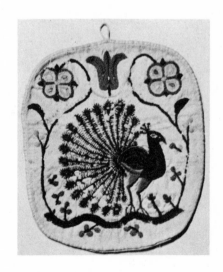

Left: Towel, embroidered in brilliant colors on old homespun, probably used for best occasions, or used as a cover. (Mr. and Mrs. Samuel Stayer Collection) Below: Miniature chest of drawers in cherry wood. The "Tauf-schein," or Baptismal Certificate above it, with elegant peacock, is dated 1787. The candlesticks are of brass, and the bowl of pewter.

113

TULIP
MOTIF

The tulip motif was one of the most frequently used designs. A few examples of widely differing objects incorporating this motif are shown here.

Above: The other side of the two-handled jar reproduced on page 112. Made by George Hubener. Left: Kettle holder decorated in crewel stitch. Below: Pine and poplar chest in blue-green with red and yellow design. (The Metropolitan Museum of Art. Gift of Mrs. Robert W. de Forest, 1933)

Right: Birth certificate from Piqua, Ohio. c. 1810 (Columbus Gallery of Fine Arts). Below: Cherry wood chest for blankets, with inlaid locust wood decoration. (Author's Collection)

Right: Candle box with painted decoration. (The Metropolitan Museum of Art. Gift of Mrs. Robert W. de Forest, 1933)

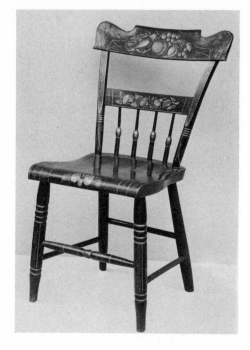

Above Left and Bottom Right: Two sides of the same Valentine. When unfolded, it displays emblems and various American sailing ships.

Above: Bride's box. (The Metropolitan Museum of Art. Gift of Mrs. Robert W. de Forest, 1933)   Top Right: Dark brown stencil pattern chair with blue-green, yellow, and gold. c. 1825. (The Metropolitan Museum of Art. Gift of Mrs. Robert W. de Forest, 1933)

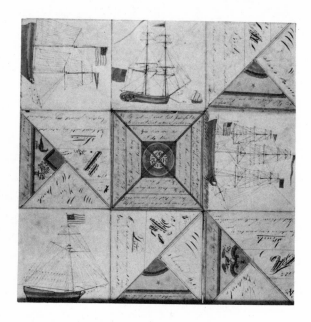

Above: Painted chest with dominant heart motif. (The Metropolitan Museum of Art. Gift of Mrs. Robert W. de Forest, 1933)   Left: Dark green chair with stencil design of gold, red, and blue.   Below: Decorated wooden box dated 1790. There are tulip designs on the sides and a typical barn symbol on the sliding lid. (Author's Collection)

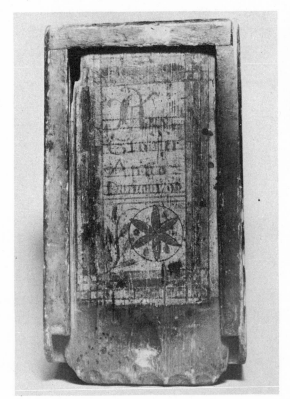

CHESTS

OF

DIFFERENT

COUNTIES

Above: Dower chest from Lebanon County with arched panels supported by columns and painted with tulips. (The Metropolitan Museum of Art. Rogers Fund, 1944)

Left: Dower chest from Berks County, with the usual unicorn and flower patterns, supplemented in this case by colonial horsemen. (The Metropolitan Museum of Art. Rogers Fund, 1923)

Below: Painted dower chest from Dauphin County attributed to Christian Selzer. (The Metropolitan Museum of Art. Gift of Mrs. Robert W. de Forest, 1933)

Left: Dower chest from Montgomery County with painted decoration and stippled bordering. (Metropolitan Museum of Art. Gift of Mrs. Robert W. de Forest, 1933)

Right: Dower chest of architectural type from Lancaster County, with moldings and pilasters. (Metropolitan Museum of Art. Gift of Mrs. Robert W. de Forest, 1933)

Below: Detail of panel from a painted chest of Lebanon County, dated 1804. (Philadelphia Museum of Art)

The chests on these pages, of the late 18th or early 19th Century, are excellent examples of the different designs for which the respective counties are famous. Lancaster, Lebanon, Lehigh, Berks, Montgomery, and Dauphin Counties each specialized in a characteristic type of chest and motif.

Above: Painted bride's box of bent wood. (The Metropolitan Museum of Art. Gift of Mrs.
Robert W. de Forest, 1933) Below: A magnificent example of the richly painted tulip and
unicorn motif of the Berks County dower chest. Dated 1784. The colors are reds, blues, and
black on white panels.

Above: Dower chest also from Berks County, with stippled back, and panels painted with the customary unicorns and tulips. (Philadelphia Museum of Art)

Right: Attractive painted cupboard containing early imported chinaware.

Left: Cookie cutter of tin with man-on-horse motif. This motif is very rare and eagerly sought by collectors. (Author's Collection)

Pie safe of tin and wood with Pennsylvania Dutch motifs. (Bigler Collection)

Above: Tin-plate foot warmer punched with various Pennsylvania Dutch motifs. The openings are both decorative and functional. (Author's Collection)

Left: Early handwoven wool and cotton coverlet in typical colors of dark blue and white. (Philadelphia Museum of Art)

Above Left: Painting made on the reverse side of glass, and framed as a picture. Late 18th Century. (Pennsylvania Farm Museum of Landis Valley) Above Right: Cast iron trivet with Pennsylvania Dutch motifs. On the back is incised "B. Rimby, Baltimore, 1841." (Osburn Collection) Below Left: Star design quilt made of diamond shaped patches, intended for a child's bed. (Mrs. Roy Brenneman Collection) Below Right: Cast metal bootjack. (Abby Aldrich Rockefeller Folk Art Collection)

Above: Four poster bed with overall stippling treatment and painted sunken panels. (Aardrup Collection)   Below Left: Decorated box with sliding lid, sometimes used for candles or spices. Below Right: Early sheet iron candlestick, made either to stand or to hang on a wall. (Pennsylvania Farm Museum of Landis Valley)

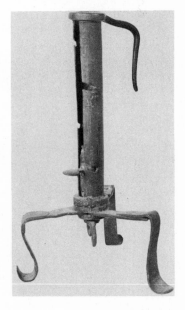

Above Left and Right: Two toilet bottles of colored Stiegel type glass. Below: Flower vase made by Charles Headman in Bucks County. Dated 1849. (Philadelphia Museum of Art)

Above: Birth certificate of 1794 from Northampton County. (Columbus Gallery of Fine Arts)
Below: Decorated chest of drawers, showing Connecticut influence in Pennsylvania Dutch work,
c. 1780. (Philadelphia Museum of Art)

Above Left: Mirror with landscape painted on reverse side of the glass. c. 1840. (Pennsylvania Farm Museum of Landis Valley)   Above Right: Earthenware pitcher, made by R. C. Remmey. Dated 1891.   Below Left: Another glass painting by an unknown artist. c. 1820.   Below Right: Brush and pen drawing inscribed "Ledy Waschingdon" and "Exselenc Georg General Waschingdon." c. 1771. (Abby Aldrich Rockefeller Folk Art Collection)

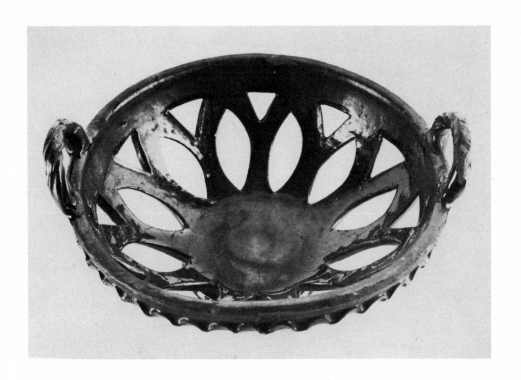

*Above: Two-handled openwork pottery bowl.
Bottom Left: Basketwork bowl and cover, in
olive green pottery. Bottom Right: Decanter of
colored Stiegel type glass. (Philadelphia Museum of Art)*

Above: Friendship quilt composed of squares executed by different individuals. The bride sewed these together into a quilt. (Mr. and Mrs. Samuel Dyke Collection) Right: Butter mold. (The Metropolitan Museum of Art. Gift of Mrs. Robert W. de Forest, 1933)

Above: This well designed specimen of a popular motif is cut from sheet iron, and was used as a weathervane. (Pennsylvania Farm Museum of Landis Valley)

Right: Iron escutcheon on the front door of Binagle's Church near Palmyra, Pennsylvania. The lock on the inside of the door is signed "Rohrer, Lebanon," which suggests that Rohrer probably made the escutcheon also. (Courtesy Binagle's Church)

Right: Certificate of unusual design, 1929. (Philadelphia Museum of Art) Below: The bed in this bedroom is decorated with a stipple pattern widely used throughout Pennsylvania. See page 60 for a close-up picture of the chest of drawers from the Mahontongo Valley. (Philadelphia Museum of Art. Photograph by A. J. Wyatt, Staff Photographer)

Above: Illumination, probably executed by a schoolmaster as a copy for children.   Below Left: Iron stag horn and rat tail hinge, a typical Pennsylvania Dutch fitting. c. 1710. (Philadelphia Museum of Art)   Below Right: Handwoven coverlet of the late 18th Century. (Philadelphia Museum of Art)

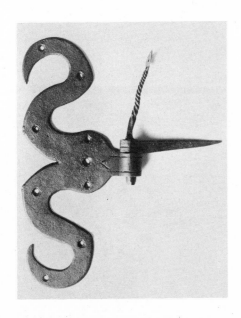

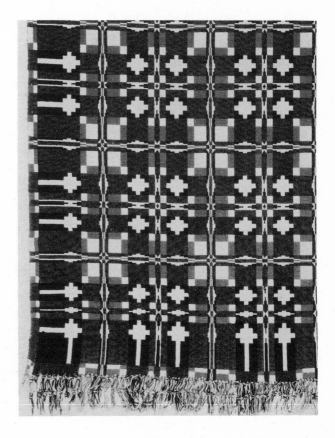

Above and Below: Two unusual pen and wash drawings inscribed 1773 and 1771 respectively.

Left: Bride's box of bent wood, with typical painted design of the bride and groom amid floral and emblematical decorations.

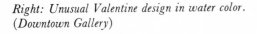

Above: Decorative calligraphy incorporating the passage, "Strait is the gate and narrow is the way which leadeth unto life, and few those be that find it." (In The Brooklyn Museum Collection)

Right: Unusual Valentine design in water color. (Downtown Gallery)

135

Above: A corner of a child's bedroom. Below: The other end of the same room. On the mantel is painted a contemporary interpretation of a Pennsylvania Dutch bird and flower motif.

The drawings on this and the next six pages have been adapted from authentic Pennsylvania Dutch motifs found on butter molds, tinware, wooden chests, pottery, barns, cookie cutters, textiles, fractur, and other objects.

This page illustrates designs derived from butter molds.

Right and Below: Two flower motifs adapted from designs on tinware.

138

Above Left: Motif from decorated wooden chest.

Above Right: Bird and flower motif used by courtesy of the Free Philadelphia Library.

Right: Double-headed eagle motif adapted from sgraffito ware plate.

These two pages illustrate Pennsylvania Dutch barn symbol motifs.

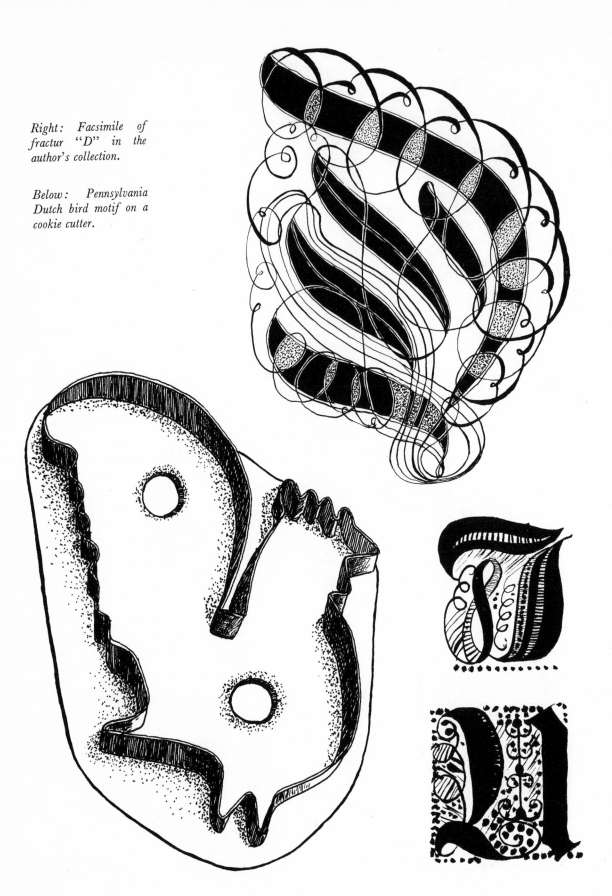

Right: Facsimile of fractur "D" in the author's collection.

Below: Pennsylvania Dutch bird motif on a cookie cutter.

All the initials on these two pages are derived from Pennsylvania Dutch fractur work.

Below: Another rooster design adapted from a cookie cutter.

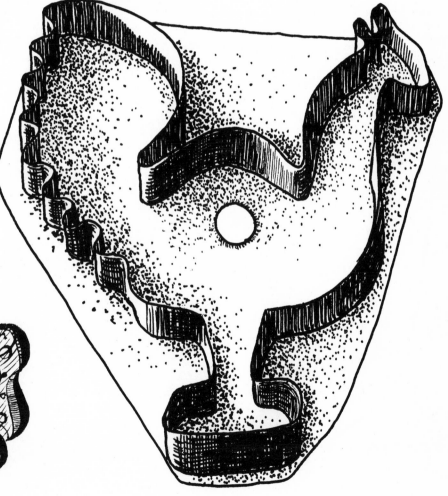

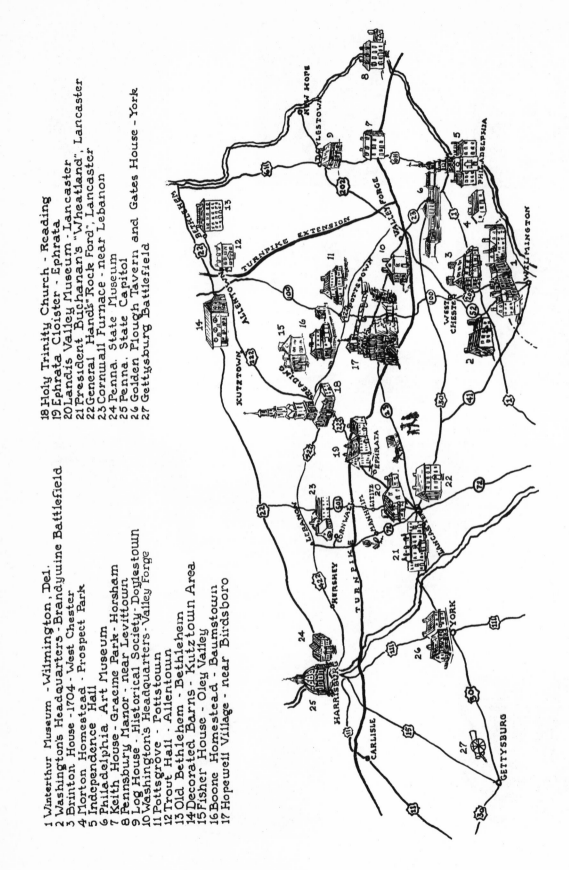

1 Winterthur Museum - Wilmington, Del.
2 Washington's Headquarters - Brandywine Battlefield
3 Brinton House - 1704 - West Chester
4 Morton Homestead - Prospect Park
5 Independence Hall
6 Philadelphia Art Museum
7 Keith House - Graeme Park - Horsham
8 Pennsbury Manor - near Levittown
9 Log House - Historical Society - Doylestown
10 Washington's Headquarters - Valley Forge
11 Pottsgrove - Pottstown
12 Trout Hall - Allentown
13 Old Bethlehem - Bethlehem
14 Decorated Barns - Kutztown Area
15 Fisher House - Oley Valley
16 Boone Homestead - Baumstown
17 Hopewell Village - near Birdsboro

18 Holy Trinity Church - Reading
19 Ephrata Cloister - Ephrata
20 Landis Valley Museum - Lancaster
21 President Buchanan's "Wheatland", Lancaster
22 General Hand's "Rock Ford", Lancaster
23 Cornwall Furnace - near Lebanon
24 Penna. State Museum
25 Penna. State Capitol
26 Golden Plough Tavern and Gates House - York
27 Gettysburg Battlefield

Tourist map of the Pennsylvania Dutch country.

BIBLIOGRAPHY

History of the Classis of Lancaster and of the Eastern Synod of the Reformed Church in the United States (1852-1940)

The History of the Lancaster Conference of the Evangelical Lutheran Ministerium of Pennsylvania and the Adjacent States together with the Histories of its Congregations.
Published by the Conference at Lebanon, Pennsylvania (1942)

Home Craft Course in Pennsylvania German Architecture
Richard Montgomery
Published by Mrs. Naaman Keyser (1945)

Tulip Ware of the Pennsylvania German Potters
Edwin Attlee Barber
The Pennsylvania Museum School of Industrial Art (1903)

The Bible in Iron
Henry C. Mercer. (Second Edition) by Horace M. Mann
The Bucks County Historical Society (1941)

Pewter in America
Leslie Irwin Laughlin
Houghton Mifflin Company (1940)

Pennsylvania Illuminated Manuscripts
Henry S. Borneman
Pennsylvania German Society (1937)

The Red Hills
Cornelius Weygandt
University of Pennsylvania Press (1929)

Pennsylvania Dutch Stuff
Earl F. Robacker
University of Pennsylvania Press (1944)

The Survival of the Mediaeval Art of Illuminative Writing Among the Pennsylvania Germans
Henry C. Mercer

Early American Gunsmiths, 1650-1850
Henry J. Kauffman
The Stackpole Company (1952)

Consider the Lilies How They Grow (Vol. II)
John Joseph Stoudt (1937)
Pennsylvania German Folklore Society

The History of Education
Elwood P. Cubberly
Houghton Mifflin Company (1920)

The Shuttle Craft Book of American Hand Weaving
Mary Meigs Atwater
The Macmillan Company (1945)

Early American Glass
Rhea Mansfield Knittle
The Century Co. (1927)

Old Iron
Philip Meredith Allen
The Antiquarian (Vol. VIII, No. 2)

The Village Tinsmith
Mabel M. Swan
Antiques Magazine (Vol. XIII, No. 3)

American Glass
George S. and Helen McKearin
Crown Publishers, Inc. (1941)

American Needlework
Georgiana Brown Harbeson
Coward–McCann, Inc. (1938)

Early American Textiles
Frances Little
D. Appleton–Century Co. (1931)

Home Craft Course in Pennsylvania German Spinning and Dyeing
Bernice B. Osburn
Mrs. Naaman Keyser (1945)

Stiegel Glass
Frederick William Hunter
Houghton Mifflin Co. (1914)

The Pennsylvania Kentucky Rifle
Henry J. Kauffman
The Stackpole Company (1960)

EARLY AMERICAN COPPER, TIN, AND BRASS
Henry J. Kauffman
Medill McBride Company (1950)

CHRISTOPHER SOWER, SR. (1694-1758)
(Printer in Germantown)
An Annotated Bibliography compiled by Felix
   Reichman
Carl Schurtz Memorial Foundation (1943)

THE GERMAN AND SWISS SETTLEMENTS OF
   COLONIAL PENNSYLVANIA
(A Study of the So-called Pennsylvania Dutch)
Oscar Kuhns
Henry Holt & Co. (1901)

THE FOUNDING OF AMERICAN CIVILIZATION
(The Middle Colonies)
Thomas Jefferson Wertenbaker
Charles Scribners & Sons (1938)

THE FURNITURE OF THE PILGRIM CENTURY
Wallace Nutting
Old America Co. (1924)

MACHINE SHOP AND FOUNDRY PROJECTS
Henry J. Kauffman
McKnight and McKnight (1959)

THE HOUSE OF THE MILLER AT MILLBACH
(The Architecture, Arts and Crafts of the
   Pennsylvania Germans)
Joseph Downs
Pennsylvania Museum of Art (1929)

THE PENNSYLVANIA GERMANS
Edited by Ralph Wood
Princeton University Press (1942)

PROCEEDINGS OF THE PENNSYLVANIA GERMAN
   SOCIETY
(Vol. XLIX)
Published by the Society

LANCASTER COUNTY, PENNSYLVANIA
(A History)
Editor-in-Chief, H.M.J. Klein
Lewis Historical Publishing Co., Inc. (1924)

THE ORIGIN OF LOG HOUSES IN THE UNITED
   STATES
Dr. Henry C. Mercer

Dover Books on Art

Art, History of Art, Antiques, Graphic Arts, Handcrafts

ART STUDENTS' ANATOMY, E. J. Farris. Outstanding art anatomy that uses chiefly living objects for its illustrations. 71 photos of undraped men, women, children are accompanied by carefully labeled matching sketches to illustrate the skeletal system, articulations and movements, bony landmarks, the muscular system, skin, fasciae, fat, etc. 9 x-ray photos show movement of joints. Undraped models are shown in such actions as serving in tennis, drawing a bow in archery, playing football, dancing, preparing to spring and to dive. Also discussed and illustrated are proportions, age and sex differences, the anatomy of the smile, etc. 8 plates by the great early 18th century anatomic illustrator Siegfried Albinus are also included. Glossary. 158 figures, 7 in color. x + 159pp. 5⅝ x 8⅜.   T744 Paperbound **$1.50**

AN ATLAS OF ANATOMY FOR ARTISTS, F Schider. A new 3rd edition of this standard text enlarged by 52 new illustrations of hands, anatomical studies by Cloquet, and expressive life studies of the body by Barcsay. 189 clear, detailed plates offer you precise information of impeccable accuracy. 29 plates show all aspects of the skeleton, with closeups of special areas, while 54 full-page plates, mostly in two colors, give human musculature as seen from four different points of view, with cutaways for important portions of the body. 14 full-page plates provide photographs of hand forms, eyelids, female breasts, and indicate the location of muscles upon models. 59 additional plates show how great artists of the past utilized human anatomy. They reproduce sketches and finished work by such artists as Michelangelo, Leonardo da Vinci, Goya, and 15 others. This is a lifetime reference work which will be one of the most important books in any artist's library. "The standard reference tool," AMERICAN LIBRARY ASSOCIATION. "Excellent," AMERICAN ARTIST. Third enlarged edition. 189 plates, 647 illustrations. xxvi + 192pp. 7⅞ x 10⅝.   T241 Clothbound **$6.00**

AN ATLAS OF ANIMAL ANATOMY FOR ARTISTS, W. Ellenberger, H. Baum, H. Dittrich. The largest, richest animal anatomy for artists available in English. 99 detailed anatomical plates of such animals as the horse, dog, cat, lion, deer, seal, kangaroo, flying squirrel, cow, bull, goat, monkey, hare, and bat. Surface features are clearly indicated, while progressive beneath-the-skin pictures show musculature, tendons, and bone structure. Rest and action are exhibited in terms of musculature and skeletal structure and detailed cross-sections are given for heads and important features. The animals chosen are representative of specific families so that a study of these anatomies will provide knowledge of hundreds of related species. "Highly recommended as one of the very few books on the subject worthy of being used as an authoritative guide," DESIGN. "Gives a fundamental knowledge," AMERICAN ARTIST. Second revised, enlarged edition with new plates from Cuvier, Stubbs, etc. 288 illustrations. 153pp. 11⅜ x 9.   T82 Clothbound **$6.00**

THE HUMAN FIGURE IN MOTION, Eadweard Muybridge. The largest selection in print of Muybridge's famous high-speed action photos of the human figure in motion. 4789 photographs illustrate 162 different actions: men, women, children—mostly undraped—are shown walking, running, carrying various objects, sitting, lying down, climbing, throwing, arising, and performing over 150 other actions. Some actions are shown in as many as 150 photographs each. All in all there are more than 500 action strips in this enormous volume, series shots taken at shutter speeds of as high as 1/6000th of a second! These are not posed shots, but true stopped motion. They show bone and muscle in situations that the human eye is not fast enough to capture. Earlier, smaller editions of these prints have brought $40 and more on the out-of-print market. "A must for artists," ART IN FOCUS. "An unparalleled dictionary of action for all artists," AMERICAN ARTIST. 390 full-page plates, with 4789 photographs. Printed on heavy glossy stock. Reinforced binding with headbands. xxi + 390pp. 7⅞ x 10⅝.
T204 Clothbound **$10.00**

ANIMALS IN MOTION, Eadweard Muybridge. This is the largest collection of animal action photos in print. 34 different animals (horses, mules, oxen, goats, camels, pigs, cats, guanacos, lions, gnus, deer, monkeys, eagles—and 21 others) in 132 characteristic actions. The horse alone is shown in more than 40 different actions. All 3919 photographs are taken in series at speeds up to 1/6000th of a second. The secrets of leg motion, spinal patterns, head movements, strains and contortions shown nowhere else are captured. You will see exactly how a lion sets his foot down; how an elephant's knees are like a human's—and how they differ; the position of a kangaroo's legs in mid-leap; how an ostrich's head bobs; details of the flight of birds—and thousands of facets of motion only the fastest cameras can catch. Photographed from domestic animals and animals in the Philadelphia zoo, it contains neither semiposed artificial shots nor distorted telephoto shots taken under adverse conditions. Artists, biologists, decorators, cartoonists, will find this book indispensable for understanding animals in motion. "A really marvelous series of plates," NATURE (London). "The dry plate's most spectacular early use was by Eadweard Muybridge," LIFE. 3919 photographs; 380 full pages of plates. 440pp. Printed on heavy glossy paper. Deluxe binding with headbands. 7⅞ x 10⅝.   T203 Clothbound **$10.00**

CATALOGUE OF DOVER BOOKS

SHAKER FURNITURE, E. D. Andrews and F. Andrews. The most illuminating study on what many scholars consider the best examples of functional furniture ever made. Includes the history of the sect and the development of Shaker style. The 48 magnificent plates show tables, chairs, cupboards, chests, boxes, desks, beds, woodenware, and much more, and are accompanied by detailed commentary. For all antique collectors and dealers, designers and decorators, historians and folklorists. "Distinguished in scholarship, in pictorial illumination, and in all the essentials of fine book making," Antiques. 3 Appendixes. Bibliography. Index. 192pp. 7⅞ x 10¾.   T679 Paperbound **$2.00**

JAPANESE HOMES AND THEIR SURROUNDINGS, E. S. Morse. Every aspect of the purely traditional Japanese home, from general plan and major structural features to ceremonial and traditional appointments—tatami, hibachi, shoji, tokonoma, etc. The most exhaustive discussion in English, this book is equally honored for its strikingly modern conception of architecture. First published in 1886, before the contamination of the Japanese traditions, it preserves the authentic features of an ideal of construction that is steadily gaining devotees in the Western world. 307 illustrations by the author. Index. Glossary. xxxvi + 372pp. 5⅝ x 8⅜.   T746 Paperbound **$2.00**

COLONIAL LIGHTING, Arthur H. Hayward. The largest selection of antique lamps ever illustrated anywhere, from rush light-holders of earliest settlers to 1880's—with main emphasis on Colonial era. Primitive attempts at illumination ("Betty" lamps, variations of open wick design, candle molds, reflectors, etc.), whale oil lamps, painted and japanned hand lamps, Sandwich glass candlesticks, astral lamps, Bennington ware and chandeliers of wood, iron, pewter, brass, crystal, bronze and silver. Hundreds of illustrations, loads of information on colonial life, customs, habits, place of acquisition of lamps illustrated. A unique, thoroughgoing survey of an interesting aspect of Americana. Enlarged (1962) edition. New Introduction by James R. Marsh. Supplement "Colonial Chandeliers," photographs with descriptive notes. 169 illustrations, 647 lamps. xxxi + 312pp. 5⅝ x 8¼.   T975 Paperbound **$2.00**

CHINESE HOUSEHOLD FURNITURE, George N. Kates. The first book-length study of authentic Chinese domestic furniture in Western language. Summarises practically everything known about Chinese furniture in pure state, uninfluenced by West. History of style, unusual woods used, craftsmanship, principles of design, specific forms like wardrobes, chests and boxes, beds, chairs, tables, stools, cupboards and other pieces. Based on author's own investigation into scanty Chinese historical sources and surviving pieces in private collections and museums. Will reveal a new dimension of simple, beautiful work to all interior decorators, furniture designers, craftsmen. 123 illustrations; 112 photographs. Bibliography. xiii + 205pp. 5¼ x 7¾.   T958 Paperbound **$1.50**

ART AND THE SOCIAL ORDER, Professor D. W. Gotshalk, University of Illinois. One of the most profound and most influential studies of aesthetics written in our generation, this work is unusual in considering art from the relational point of view, as a transaction consisting of creation-object-apprehension. Discussing material from the fine arts, literature, music, and related disciplines, it analyzes the aesthetic experience, fine art, the creative process, art materials, form, expression, function, art criticism, art and social life and living. Graceful and fluent in expression, it requires no previous background in aesthetics and will be read with considerable enjoyment by anyone interested in the theory of art. "Clear, interesting, the soundest and most penetrating work in recent years," C. J. Ducasse, Brown University. New preface by Professor Gotshalk. xvi + 248pp. 5⅝ x 8½.
                                                                           T294 Paperbound **$1.50**

FOUNDATIONS OF MODERN ART, A. Ozenfant. An illuminating discussion by a great artist of the interrelationship of all forms of human creativity, from painting to science, writing to religion. The creative process is explored in all facets of art, from paleolithic cave painting to modern French painting and architecture, and the great universals of art are isolated. Expressing its countless insights in aphorisms accompanied by carefully selected illustrations, this book is itself an embodiment in prose of the creative process. Enlarged by 4 new chapters. 226 illustrations. 368pp. 6⅛ x 9¼.   T215 Paperbound **$1.95**

VITRUVIUS: TEN BOOKS ON ARCHITECTURE. Book by 1st century Roman architect, engineer, is oldest, most influential work on architecture in existence; for hundreds of years his specific instructions were followed all over the world, by such men as Bramante, Michelangelo, Palladio, etc., and are reflected in major buildings. He describes classic principles of symmetry, harmony; design of treasury, prison, etc.; methods of durability; much more. He wrote in a fascinating manner, and often digressed to give interesting sidelights, making this volume appealing reading even to the non-professional. Standard English translation, by Prof. M. H. Morgan, Harvard U. Index. 6 illus. 334pp. 5⅜ x 8.   T645 Paperbound **$2.00**

THE BROWN DECADES, Lewis Mumford. In this now classic study of the arts in America, Lewis Mumford resurrects the "buried renaissance" of the post-Civil War period. He demonstrates that it contained the seeds of a new integrity and power and documents his study with detailed accounts of the founding of modern architecture in the work of Sullivan, Richardson, Root, Roebling; landscape development of Marsh, Olmstead, and Eliot; the graphic arts of Homer, Eakins, and Ryder. 2nd revised enlarged edition. Bibliography. 12 illustrations. Index. xiv + 266pp. 5⅜ x 8.   T200 Paperbound **$1.65**

CATALOGUE OF DOVER BOOKS

ART ANATOMY, William Rimmer, M.D. Often called one of America's foremost contributions to art instruction, a work of art in its own right. More than 700 line drawings by the author, first-rate anatomist and dissector as well as artist, with a non-technical anatomical text. Impeccably accurate drawings of muscles, skeletal structure, surface features, other aspects of males and females, children, adults and aged persons show not only form, size, insertion and articulation but personality and emotion as reflected by physical features usually ignored in modern anatomical works. Complete unabridged reproduction of 1876 edition slightly rearranged. Introduction by Robert Hutchinson. 722 illustrations. xiii + 153pp. 7¾ x 10¾.
T908 Paperbound **$2.00**

ANIMAL DRAWING: ANATOMY AND ACTION FOR ARTISTS, C. R. Knight. The author and illustrator of this work was "the most distinguished painter of animal life." This extensive course in animal drawing discusses musculature, bone structure, animal psychology, movements, habits, habitats. Innumerable tips on proportions, light and shadow play, coloring, hair formation, feather arrangement, scales, how animals lie down, animal expressions, etc., from great apes to birds. Pointers on avoiding gracelessness in horses, deer; on introducing proper power and bulk to heavier animals; on giving proper grace and subtle expression to members of the cat family. Originally titled "Animal Anatomy and Psychology for the Artist and Layman." Over 123 illustrations. 149pp. 8¼ x 10½.
T426 Paperbound **$2.00**

DESIGN FOR ARTISTS AND CRAFTSMEN, L. Wolchonok. The most thorough course ever prepared on the creation of art motifs and designs. It teaches you to create your own designs out of things around you — from geometric patterns, plants, birds, animals, humans, landscapes, and man-made objects. It leads you step by step through the creation of more than 1300 designs, and shows you how to create design that is fresh, well-founded, and original. Mr. Wolchonok, whose text is used by scores of art schools, shows you how the same idea can be developed into many different forms, ranging from near representationalism to the most advanced forms of abstraction. The material in this book is entirely new, and combines full awareness of traditional design with the work of such men as Miro, Léger, Picasso, Moore, and others. 113 detailed exercises, with instruction hints, diagrams, and details to enable you to apply Wolchonok's methods to your own work. "A great contribution to the field of design and crafts," N. Y. SOCIETY OF CRAFTSMEN. More than 1300 illustrations. xv + 207pp. 7⅞ x 10¾.
T274 Clothbound **$4.95**

HAWTHORNE ON PAINTING. A vivid recreation, from students' notes, of instruction by Charles W. Hawthorne, given for over 31 years at his famous Cape Cod School of Art. Divided into sections on the outdoor model, still life, landscape, the indoor model, and water color, each section begins with a concise essay, followed by epigrammatic comments on color, form, seeing, etc. Not a formal course, but comments of a great teacher-painter on specific student works, which will solve problems in your own painting and understanding of art. "An excellent introduction for laymen and students alike," Time. Introduction. 100pp. 5⅜ x 8.
T653 Paperbound **$1.00**

THE ENJOYMENT AND USE OF COLOR, Walter Sargent. This book explains fascinating relations among colors, between colors in nature and art; describes experiments that you can perform to understand these relations more thoroughly; points out hundreds of little known facts about color values, intensities, effects of high and low illumination, complementary colors, color harmonies. Practical hints for painters, references to techniques of masters, questions at chapter ends for self-testing all make this a valuable book for artists, professional and amateur, and for general readers interested in world of color. Republication of 1923 edition. 35 illustrations, 6 full-page plates. New color frontispiece. Index. xii + 274pp. 5⅜ x 8.
T944 Paperbound **$2.25**

DECORATIVE ALPHABETS AND INITIALS, ed. by Alexander Nesbitt. No payment, no permission needed to reproduce any one of these 3924 different letters, covering 1000 years. Crisp, clear letters all in line, from Anglo-Saxon mss., Luebeck Cathedral, 15th century Augsburg; the work of Dürer, Holbein, Cresci, Beardsley, Rossing Wadsworth, John Moylin, etc. Every imaginable style. 91 complete alphabets. 123 full-page plates. 192pp. 7¾ x 10¾.
T544 Paperbound **$2.25**

THREE CLASSICS OF ITALIAN CALLIGRAPHY, edited by Oscar Ogg. Here, combined in a single volume, are complete reproductions of three famous calligraphic works written by the greatest writing masters of the Renaissance: Arrighi's OPERINA and IL MODO, Tagliente's LO PRESENTE LIBRO, and Palatino's LIBRO NUOVO. These books present more than 200 complete alphabets and thousands of lettered specimens. The basic hand is Papal Chancery, but scores of other alphabets are also given: European and Asiatic local alphabets, foliated and art alphabets, scrolls, cartouches, borders, etc. Text is in Italian. Introduction. 245 plates. x + 272pp. 6⅛ x 9¼.
T212 Paperbound **$2.25**

CALLIGRAPHY, J. G. Schwandner. One of the legendary books in the graphic arts, copies of which brought $500 each on the rare book market, now reprinted for the first time in over 200 years. A beautiful plate book of graceful calligraphy, and an inexhaustible source of first-rate material copyright-free, for artists, and directors, craftsmen, commercial artists, etc. More than 300 ornamental initials forming 12 complete alphabets, over 150 ornate frames and panels, over 200 flourishes, over 75 calligraphic pictures including a temple, cherubs, cocks, dodos, stags, chamois, foliated lions, greyhounds, etc. Thousand of calligraphic elements to be used for suggestions of quality, sophistication, antiquity, and sheer beauty. Historical introduction. 158 full-page plates. 368pp. 9 x 13.
T475 Clothbound **$10.00**

CATALOGUE OF DOVER BOOKS

THE HISTORY AND TECHNIQUE OF LETTERING, A. Nesbitt. The only thorough inexpensive history of letter forms from the point of view of the artist. Mr. Nesbitt covers every major development in lettering from the ancient Egyptians to the present and illustrates each development with a complete alphabet. Such masters as Baskerville, Bell, Bodoni, Caslon, Koch, Kilian, Morris, Garamont, Jenson, and dozens of others are analyzed in terms of artistry and historical development. The author also presents a 65-page practical course in lettering, besides the full historical text. 89 complete alphabets; 165 additional lettered specimens. xvii + 300pp. 5⅜ x 8. T427 Paperbound **$2.00**

FOOT-HIGH LETTERS: A GUIDE TO LETTERING (A PRACTICAL SYLLABUS FOR TEACHERS), M. Price. A complete alphabet of Classic Roman letters, each a foot high, each on a separate 16 x 22 plate—perfect for use in lettering classes. In addition to an accompanying description, each plate also contains 9 two-inch-high forms of letter in various type faces, such as "Caslon," "Empire," "Onyx," and "Neuland," illustrating the many possible derivations from the standard classical forms. One plate contains 21 additional forms of the letter A. The fully illustrated 16-page syllabus by Mr. Price, formerly of the Pratt Institute and the Rhode Island School of Design, contains dozens of useful suggestions for student and teacher alike. An indispensable teaching aid. Extensively revised. 16-page syllabus and 30 plates in slip cover, 16 x 22. T239 Clothbound **$6.00**

THE STYLES OF ORNAMENT, Alexander Speltz. Largest collection of ornaments in print— 3765 illustrations of prehistoric, Lombard, Gothic, Frank, Romanesque, Mohammedan, Renaissance, Polish, Swiss, Rococo, Sheraton, Empire, U. S. Colonial, etc., ornament. Gargoyles, dragons, columns, necklaces, urns, friezes, furniture, buildings, keyholes, tapestries, fantastic animals, armor, religious objects, much more, all in line. Reproduce any one free. Index. Bibliography. 400 plates. 656pp. 5⅝ x 8⅜. T557 Paperbound **$2.35**

HANDBOOK OF DESIGNS AND DEVICES, C. P. Hornung. This unique book is indispensable to the designer, commercial artist, and hobbyist. It is not a textbook but a working collection of 1836 basic designs and variations, carefully reproduced, which may be used without permission. Variations of circle, line, band, triangle, square, cross, diamond, swastika, pentagon, octagon, hexagon, star, scroll, interlacement, shields, etc. Supplementary notes on the background and symbolism of the figures. "A necessity to every designer who would be original without having to labor heavily," ARTIST AND ADVERTISER. 204 plates. 240pp. 5⅜ x 8. T125 Paperbound **$1.90**

THE UNIVERSAL PENMAN, George Bickham. This beautiful book, which first appeared in 1743, is the largest collection of calligraphic specimens, flourishes, alphabets, and calligraphic illustrations ever published. 212 full-page plates are drawn from the work of such 18th century masters of English roundhand as Dove, Champion, Bland, and 20 others. They contain 22 complete alphabets, over 2,000 flourishes, and 122 illustrations, each drawn with a stylistic grace impossible to describe. This book is invaluable to anyone interested in the beauties of calligraphy, or to any artist, hobbyist, or craftsman who wishes to use the very best ornamental handwriting and flourishes for decorative purposes. Commercial artists, advertising artists, have found it unexcelled as a source of material suggesting quality. "An essential part of any art library, and a book of permanent value," AMERICAN ARTIST. 212 plates. 224pp. 9 x 13¾. T20 Clothbound **$10.00**

1800 WOODCUTS BY THOMAS BEWICK AND HIS SCHOOL. Prepared by Dover's editorial staff, this is the largest collection of woodcuts by Bewick and his school ever compiled. Contains the complete engravings from all his major works and a wide range of illustrations from lesser-known collections, all photographed from clear copies of the original books and reproduced in line. Carefully and conveniently organized into sections on Nature (animals and birds, scenery and landscapes, plants, insects, etc.), People (love and courtship, social life, school and domestic scenes, misfortunes, costumes, etc.), Business and Trade, and illustrations from primers, fairytales, spelling books, frontispieces, borders, fables and allegories, etc. In addition to technical proficiency and simple beauty, Bewick's work is remarkable as a mode of pictorial symbolism, reflecting rustic tranquility, an atmosphere of rest, simplicity, idyllic contentment. A delight for the eye, an inexhaustible source of illustrative material for art studios, commercial artists, advertising agencies. Individual illustrations (up to 10 for any one use) are copyright free. Classified index. Bibliography and sources. Introduction by Robert Hutchinson. 1800 woodcuts. xiv + 247pp. 9 x 12. T766 Clothbound **$10.00**

A HANDBOOK OF EARLY ADVERTISING ART, C. P. Hornung. The largest collection of copyright-free early advertising art ever compiled. Vol. I contains some 2,000 illustrations of agricultural devices, animals, old automobiles, birds, buildings, Christmas decorations (with 7 Santa Clauses by Nast), allegorical figures, fire engines, horses and vehicles, Indians, portraits, sailing ships, trains, sports, trade cuts — and 30 other categories! Vol. II, devoted to typography, has over 4000 specimens: 600 different Roman, Gothic, Barnum, Old English faces; 630 ornamental type faces; 1115 initials, hundreds of scrolls, flourishes, etc. This third edition is enlarged by 78 additional plates containing all new material. "A remarkable collection," PRINTERS' INK. "A rich contribution to the history of American design," GRAPHIS. Volume I, Pictorial. Over 2000 illustrations. xiv + 242pp. 9 x 12. T122 Clothbound **$10.00** Volume II, Typographical. Over 4000 specimens. vii + 312pp. 9 x 12. T123 Clothbound **$10.00** Two volume set, T121 Clothbound, only **$18.50**

CATALOGUE OF DOVER BOOKS

METALWORK AND ENAMELLING, H. Maryon. This is probably the best book ever written on the subject. Prepared by Herbert Maryon, F.S.A., of the British Museum, it tells everything necessary for home manufacture of jewelry, rings, ear pendants, bowls, and dozens of other objects. Clearly written chapters provide precise information on such topics as materials, tools, soldering, filigree, setting stones, raising patterns, spinning metal, repoussé work, hinges and joints, metal inlaying, damascening, overlaying, niello, Japanese alloys, enamelling, cloisonné, painted enamels, casting, polishing, coloring, assaying, and dozens of other techniques. This is the next best thing to apprenticeship to a master metalworker. 363 photographs and figures. 374pp. 5½ x 8½. T183 Clothbound **$8.00**

SILK SCREEN TECHNIQUES, J. I. Biegeleisen, Max A. Cohn. A complete-to-the-last-detail copiously illustrated home course in this fast growing modern art form. Full directions for building silk screen out of inexpensive materials; explanations of five basic methods of stencil preparation—paper, blockout, tusche, film, photographic—and effects possible: light and shade, washes, dry brush, oil paint type impastos, gouaches, pastels. Detailed coverage of multicolor printing, illustrated by proofs showing the stages of a 4 color print. Special section on common difficulties. 149 illustrations, 8 in color. Sources of supply. xiv + 187pp. 6⅛ x 9¼. T433 Paperbound **$1.55**

A HANDBOOK OF WEAVES, G. H. Oelsner. Now back in print! Probably the most complete book of weaves ever printed, fully explained, differentiated, and illustrated. Includes plain weaves; irregular, double-stitched, and filling satins; derivative, basket, and rib weaves; steep, undulating, broken, offset, corkscrew, interlocking, herringbone, and fancy twills; honeycomb, lace, and crepe weaves; tricot, matelassé, and montagnac weaves; and much more. Translated and revised by S. S. Dale, with supplement on the analysis of weaves and fabrics. 1875 illustrations. vii + 402pp. 6 x 9¼. T209 Clothbound **$5.00**

BASIC BOOKBINDING, A. W. Lewis. Enables the beginner and the expert to apply the latest and most simplified techniques to rebinding old favorites and binding new paperback books. Complete lists of all necessary materials and guides to the selection of proper tools, paper, glue, boards, cloth, leather, or sheepskin covering fabrics, lettering inks and pigments, etc. You are shown how to collate a book, sew it, back it, trim it, make boards and attach them in easy step-by-step stages. Author's preface. 261 illustrations with appendix. Index. xi + 144pp. 5⅜ x 8. T169 Paperbound **$1.35**

BASKETRY, F. J. Christopher. Basic introductions cover selection of materials, use and care of tools, equipment. Easy-to-follow instructions for preparation of oval, oblong trays, lidded baskets, rush mats, tumbler holders, bicycle baskets, waste paper baskets, many other useful, beautiful articles made of coiled and woven reed, willow, rushes, raffia. Special sections present in clear, simple language and numerous illustrations all the how-to information you could need: linings, skein wire, varieties of stitching, simplified construction of handles, dying processes. For beginner and skilled craftsman alike. Edited by Majorie O'Shaugnessy. Bibliography. Sources of supply. Index. 112 illustrations. 108pp. 5 x 7¼. T903 Paperbound **75¢**

THE ART OF ETCHING, E. S. Lumsden. Everything you need to know to do etching yourself. First two sections devoted to technique of etching and engraving, covering such essentials as relative merits of zinc and copper, cleaning and grounding plates, gravers, acids, arrangement of etching-room, methods of biting, types of inks and oils, mounting, stretching and framing, preserving and restoring plates, size and color of printing papers, much more. A review of the history of the art includes separate chapters on Dürer and Lucas van Leyden, Rembrandt and Van Dyck, Goya, Meryon, Haden and Whistler, British masters of nineteenth century, modern etchers. Final section is a collection of prints by contemporary etchers with comments by the artists. Professional etchers and engravers will find this a highly useful source of examples. Beginners and teachers, students of art and printing will find it a valuable tool. Index. 208 illustrations. 384pp. 5⅜ x 8. T49 Paperbound **$2.50**

WHITTLING AND WOODCARVING, E. J. Tangerman. What to make and how to make it for even a moderately handy beginner. One of the few works that bridge gap between whittling and serious carving. History of the art, background information on selection and use of woods, grips, types of strokes and cuts, handling of tools and chapters on rustic work, flat toys and windmills, puzzles, chains, ships in bottle, nested spheres, fans, more than 100 useful, entertaining objects. Second half covers carving proper: woodcuts, low relief, sculpture in the round, lettering, inlay and marquetry, indoor and outdoor decorations, pierced designs, much more. Final chapter describes finishing, care of tools. Sixth edition. Index. 464 illustrations. x + 239pp. 5½ x 8⅛. T965 Paperbound **$1.75**

THE PRACTICE OF TEMPERA PAINTING, Daniel V. Thompson, Jr. A careful exposition of all aspects of tempera painting, including sections on many possible modern uses, propensities of various woods, choice of material for panel, making and applying the gesso, pigments and brushes, technique of the actual painting, gilding and so on—everything one need know to try a hand at this proven but neglected art. The author is unquestionably the world's leading authority on tempera methods and processes and his treatment is based on exhaustive study of manuscript material. Drawings and diagrams increase clarity of text. No one interested in tempera painting can afford to be without this book. Appendix, "Tempera Practice in Yale Art School," by Lewis E. York. 85 illustrations by York; 4 full-page plates. ix x 149pp. 5⅜ x 8½. T343 Paperbound **$1.50**

CATALOGUE OF DOVER BOOKS

DESIGN MOTIFS OF ANCIENT MEXICO, J. Enciso. This unique collection of pre-Columbian stamps for textiles and pottery contains 766 superb designs from Aztec, Olmec, Totonac, Maya, and Toltec origins. Plumed serpents, calendrical elements, wind gods, animals, flowers, demons, dancers, monsters, abstract ornament, and other designs. More than 90% of these illustrations are completely unobtainable elsewhere. Use this work to bring new barbaric beauty into your crafts or drawing. Originally $17.50. Printed in three colors. 766 illustrations, thousands of motifs. 192pp. 7⅞ x 10¾.
T84 Paperbound **$1.85**

DECORATIVE ART OF THE SOUTHWEST INDIANS, D. S. Sides. A magnificent album of authentic designs (both pre- and post-Conquest) from the pottery, textiles, and basketry of the Navaho, Hopi, Mohave, Santo Domingo, and over 20 other Southwestern groups. Designs include birds, clouds, butterflies, quadrupeds, geometric forms, etc. A valuable book for folklorists, and a treasury for artists, designers, advertisers, and craftsmen, who may use without payment or permission any of the vigorous, colorful, and strongly rhythmic designs. Aesthetic and archeological notes. 50 plates. Bibliography of over 50 items. xviii + 101pp. 5⅝ x 8⅜.
T139 Paperbound **$1.00**

PAINTING IN THE FAR EAST, Laurence Binyon. Excellent introduction by one of greatest authorities on subject studies 1500 years of oriental art (China, Japan; also Tibet, Persia), over 250 painters. Examines works, schools, influence of Wu Tao-tzu, Kanaoka, Toba Sojo, Masanobu, Okio, etc.; early traditions; Kamakura epoch; the Great Decorators; T'ang Dynasty; Matabei, beginnings of genre; Japanese woodcut, color print; much more, all chronological, in cultural context. 42 photos. Bibliography. 317pp. 6 x 9¼.
T520 Paperbound **$2.00**

ON THE LAWS OF JAPANESE PAINTING, H. Bowie. This unusual book, based on 9 years of profound study-experience in the Late Kano art of Japan, remains the most authentic guide in English to the spirit and technique of Japanese painting. A wealth of interesting and useful data on control of the brush; practise exercises; manufacture of ink, brushes, colors; the use of various lines and dots to express moods. It is the best possible substitute for a series of lessons from a great oriental master. 66 plates with 220 illustrations. Index. xv + 177pp. 6⅛ x 9¼.
T30 Paperbound **$1.95**

THE MATERIALS AND TECHNIQUES OF MEDIEVAL PAINTING, D. V. Thompson. Based on years of study of medieval manuscripts and laboratory analysis of medieval paintings, this book discusses carriers and grounds, binding media, pigments, metals used in painting, etc. Considers relative merits of painting al fresco and al secco, the procession of coloring materials, burnishing, and many other matters. Preface by Bernard Berenson. Index. 239pp. 5⅜ x 8.
T327 Paperbound **$1.85**

THE CRAFTSMAN'S HANDBOOK, Cennino Cennini. This is considered the finest English translation of IL LIBRO DELL' ARTE, a 15th century Florentine introduction to art technique. It is both fascinating reading and a wonderful mirror of another culture for artists, art students, historians, social scientists, or anyone interested in details of life some 500 years ago. While it is not an exact recipe book, it gives directions for such matters as tinting papers, gilding stone, preparation of various hues of black, and many other useful but nearly forgotten facets of the painter's art. As a human document reflecting the ideas of a practising medieval artist it is particularly important. 4 illustrations. xxvii + 142pp. D. V. Thompson translator. 6⅛ x 9¼.
T54 Paperbound **$1.25**

VASARI ON TECHNIQUE, G. Vasari. Pupil of Michelangelo and outstanding biographer of the Renaissance artists, Vasari also wrote this priceless treatise on the technical methods of the painters, architects, and sculptors of his day. This is the only English translation of this practical, informative, and highly readable work. Scholars, artists, and general readers will welcome these authentic discussions of marble statues, bronze casting, fresco painting, oil painting, engraving, stained glass, rustic fountains and grottoes, etc. Introduction and notes by G. B. Brown. Index. 18 plates, 11 figures. xxiv + 328pp. 5⅜ x 8.
T717 Paperbound **$2.00**

Dover publishes books on art, music, philosophy, literature, languages, history, social sciences, psychology, handcrafts, orientalia, puzzles and entertainments, chess, pets and gardens, books explaining science, intermediate and higher mathematics, mathematical physics, engineering, biological sciences, earth sciences, classics of science, etc. Write to:

Dept. catrr.
Dover Publications, Inc.
180 Varick Street, N. Y. 14, N. Y.